AVOIDANT ATTACHMENT STYLE GUIDE & WORKBOOK

The Blueprint To Dismantle Your Emotional Fortress, Unlock Fearless Vulnerability & Build An Empire Of Unshakeable Love

Disclaimer

This book is intended for informational purposes only and should not be considered a substitute for professional therapeutic treatment. While every effort has been made to ensure the accuracy and reliability of the information presented, neither the author, publisher, nor any associated advisers or contractors assume any responsibility for the actions or decisions of readers based on the content herein. Readers are advised to consult with qualified mental health professionals for personalized advice or treatment. By engaging with this material, you acknowledge that the author, publisher, and all parties involved in the creation and distribution of this work are indemnified against any liability arising from your use or misuse of the information contained within.

Copyright © 2024 by LearnWell Books.

All rights reserved. No part of this publication may be reproduced, distributed, or transmitted in any form or by any means, including photocopying, recording, or other electronic or mechanical methods, without the prior written permission of the publisher, except in the case of brief quotations embodied in critical reviews and certain other noncommercial uses permitted by copyright law.

References to historical events, real people, or real places are often fictitious. In such cases, the names, characters, and places are products of the author's imagination. We do this where it's important to protect the privacy of people, places, and things.

689 Burke Rd
Camberwell Victoria 3124
Australia

www.LearnWellBooks.com

We're led by God. Our business is also committed to supporting kids' charities. At the time of printing, we have donated well over $100,000 to enable mentoring services for underprivileged children. By choosing our books, you are helping children who desperately need it. Thank you.

This Is Really Important.
It's a Sincere Thank You.

My name is Wayne, the founder of LearnWell.

My Dad put a book in my hands when I was 13. It was written by Zig Ziglar and it changed the course of my life. Since then, it's been books that have helped me get over breakups, learn how to be a good friend, study the lives of good people and books have been the source of my persistence through some pretty challenging times.

My purpose is now to return the favor. To create books that might be the turning point in the lives of people around the world, just like they've been for me. It's enough to almost bring me to tears to think of you holding this book, seeking information and wisdom from something that I've helped to create. I'm moved in a way that I can't fully explain.

We're a small and 'beyond-enthusiastic' team here at LearnWell. We're writers, editors, researchers, designers, formatters (oh ... and a bookkeeper!) who take your decision to learn with us incredibly seriously. We consider it a privilege to be part of your learning journey. Thank you for allowing us to join you.

If there's anything we did really well, anything we messed up, or anything AT ALL that we could do better, would you please write to us and tell us (like, right now!) We would love to hear from you!

readers@learnwellbooks.com

We're sending you our thanks, our love and our very best wishes.

Wayne
and the team at LearnWell Books.

THERAPIST APPROVED

It's our intention to produce the best books in the world on the topics we choose to write about.

Given that Attachment Theory forms the cornerstone of contemporary relationship therapy, we recognized the importance of grounding our work in validated therapeutic principles and professional expertise.

Erin Knebel, LCSW

As part of our commitment to accuracy and clinical integrity, we are grateful to Erin Knebel, a distinguished therapist specializing in attachment-based relationship therapy.

Her expert review of the manuscript and valuable feedback have enhanced the precision and therapeutic value of this work.

We appreciate her contributions in ensuring this book reflects current clinical understanding of relationship attachment dynamics.

WELCOME TO OUR COMMUNITY

"It's like a private online book club"

Imagine if you could actually meet and talk with other readers of this book and share your experiences.

Imagine if you could chat with the author or join them on a live Q&A!

Imagine getting access to the author's notes and other exclusive, unpublished material.

You can do all of that and a lot more in the LearnWell Online Community!!

- → Download your **Workbook**
- → Chat directly with the author!
- → Meet and feel supported by other readers and their experiences.
- → Access additional, exclusive content about this topic and others.
- → Join our live Author Q&A sessions online.
- → Learn faster, make lasting changes, and have 10 times more fun!

This is part of our commitment to creating the best learning resources in the world.

Scan the QR code to get FREE access
www.learnwellbooks.com/safetolove

To Sammy

You do deserve love.

I hope one day you'll find the courage to let it in.

CONTENTS

Introduction   10

PART 1: WHAT'S THE PROBLEM ANYWAY?   15

1   My Avoidant Journey   16
From Isolation To Connection. From Lonely To Loved

2   Understanding Avoidant Attachment   26
The Science Behind Our Fears

PART 2: DISMANTLING THE WALL OF DETACHMENT   45

3   A Detached Mindset: Rewiring My Avoidant Brain   46
How I Used Neuroplasticity To Create Secure Love

4   Dismissive Emotions: Learning To Speak 'Emotion'   62
A Former Avoidants Guide

5   Deactivating Behaviors: Recognizing The Patterns   76
Catching Yourself In The Act

6	The Courage To Be Vulnerable	91
	My First Steps Towards Opening Up	
7	Intimacy Bootcamp	107
	How I Learned To Stop Fearing And Love Closeness	

PART 3: A LASTING CHANGE   121

8	Independence And Interdependence	122
	Being Me While Being Together	
9	Setbacks And Healing	140
	Old Habits Die Hard	
10	Beyond Myself	158
	Supporting Our Partners And Loved Ones	

Conclusion   177

References   179

YOUR WORKBOOK

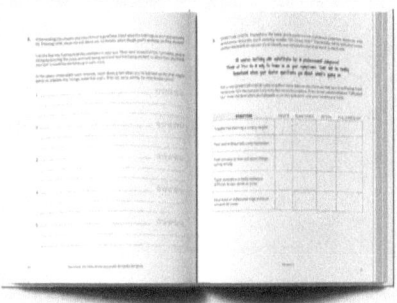

A shocking truth was discovered by a study done in 1987 – **people only remember 10% of what they read!**

That seems so discouraging.

But here's the **GOOD NEWS** – reading is **NEVER** a waste of time. As long as you do **one** important thing ...

The same study (by National Training Laboratories) shows that you will remember 90% of what you read when you **put your new knowledge into action**!

Here at LearnWell, we aim to create **the world's best learning resources**. So, we have included a highly engaging **Workbook** that helps you put your new knowledge into fun, practical action.

So, make sure you download your **FREE Workbook.** You'll find it located inside the **LearnWell Community.** Simply scan the QR code below for access.

Get your Workbook in the LearnWell Community
Scan the QR Code for access or go to:
www.learnwellbooks.com/safetolove

INTRODUCTION

I've hurt people, but it was never intentional. I hadn't heard of attachment styles until it was too late. My longest-lasting relationship before therapy ended in failure and regret. But even after I'd gone to therapy, learned about avoidant attachment, and successfully built up a healthy marriage, I still managed to destroy my relationship. I was helplessly avoidant, and it ruined my life. But my life didn't stay ruined, and I'm here to tell you how I turned things around.

Being avoidantly attached has earned a reputation for being "incurable" in online social circles. I've seen narratives about us that felt insulting and discouraging, saying things like "They'll never change", "Avoidants don't care," and "If they can't feel love, what do they have to fight for?" I'm here to tell you that these comments are ignorant. I've studied the avoidant experience, and after many brutal failures (and much therapy), I've realized the answer to our problems:

Being avoidant is not a lack of care but rather a lack of capacity.

We care a lot. However, we've been hurt in the past and our avoidant tendencies keep us safe. It's not that we don't want connection, rather we don't have the capacity for all the intense emotions, conflict, and vulnerability that a healthy relationship entails. We feel better off alone or at a safe emotional distance. That is not a fixed problem. Capacity can expand.

The things holding us back from fulfilling relationships are plastic. They are things we can work with and mold to allow for more. But I'm not going to push you. As avoidantly attached people, we need a unique approach to growth. We must lean into our needs and allow ourselves the independence, alone-time, and self-soothing space required to feel our best.

I'm not here to tell you how wrong you are for being avoidant. I'm here to help you mold avoidant attachment into something that keeps you both safe *and* connected. The solutions I share throughout this book are supportive of YOU. They're not trying to make you someone you're not.

There are 3 Parts to this book, each with a vital purpose for your journey. They include:

PART 1: WHAT'S THE PROBLEM ANYWAY?

To start, I'll lead you through my avoidant journey, and how I came to find secure love, where my avoidant tendencies were able to melt away in the safety of it. Then, we'll explore the scientific understanding of avoidant attachment, and the model for our main problem: The Wall Of Detachment.

PART 2: BREAKING THE WALL OF DETACHMENT

After understanding how The Wall Of Detachment keeps a barrier between us and secure love, Part 2 will address each layer of the wall with a single solution:

- Layer 1: A Detached Mindset –
  Solution 1: Build A Secure Mindset

- Layer 2: Dismissive Emotions –
  Solution 2: Nurture Emotional Health

- Layer 3: Deactivating Behaviors –
  Solution 3: Recognize Patterns And Reactivate

- Layer 4: Doubtful Vulnerability –
  Solution 4: Overcome Doubt To Open Up

- Layer 5: Distant Intimacy –
  Solution 5: Cultivate Closeness

Once we've applied the solutions for dissolving each layer of The Wall Of Detachment, we'll discuss how to make our progress last.

PART 3: A LASTING CHANGE

To see a lasting change in our relationships and personal fulfillment, there are a few things we will address in Part 3, including:

- How to maintain autonomy in a healthy relationship.

- How to cope with setbacks and the ups and downs of healing.

- How to include our partners, manage conflict, and forge connections in a sustainable way for someone healing avoidant attachment.

After applying everything I'll share throughout this book, my life is undeniably better. I used to think connection could only go

Introduction

so far before it became a waste of time. But now my beautiful, fulfilling marriage—which has survived moving in together, having children, and major life events—is a testimony to the heights an avoidantly attached person can reach in relationships. However, it came with a willingness to be real with myself and honest with others about my avoidance.

How willing are you?

If you can muster the courage to face a few demons, turn a new leaf, and pursue the unknown in relationships, I promise your life will transform. True connection is not some insignificant aspect of life. It is the epitome of a good life.

Connection and secure relationships can open up the world right in front of us. They can lead to great things, much joy, and better health. Are you ready for that? Then don't wait. Turn the page now and join me in Chapter 1, where you will get the full picture of where I started and how I wound up here with you.

PART 1

WHAT'S THE PROBLEM ANYWAY?

1

MY AVOIDANT JOURNEY

**From Isolation To Connection.
From Lonely To Loved**

"When you lose a possession, you realize that you valued it too much. When you lose a person, you realize that you didn't value them enough."

– Neil Strauss

MY ATTACHMENT STORY: THE PARADOX OF AVOIDANCE

The ring box clipped shut. I'll never forget that sound, even above the drumming of ocean waves. There was a moment of intensity that washed over his face. He got up slowly, brushing the sand from his knee. Immediately, I wondered whether I'd made a mistake. It was the perfect proposal, one I'd always dreamed of. But when he asked me to marry him, the brilliant hues on the horizon seemed to fade.

I spent years wondering why I said no.

Our 2-year relationship was the best I'd ever had. It felt warm and good, and I often found myself daydreaming about engagement. We spoke about marriage from time to time, but it was always in a fun and almost joking way. Still, a part of me hoped it would happen. It had taken me so long to find "the one" and stick it out. We'd crossed many milestones together before this point, and looking back, marriage was the next logical step. But when the ring came out, and I saw the intense love in his eyes, it all felt very wrong.

We walked back to the car – together but completely disconnected. I couldn't bear to look at him for a second. I didn't comfort him or try to explain. We just walked in silence, making the space between us feel like miles. In the car, he cleared his throat often. I knew this meant he was trying not to cry but failing. I stared out the window and wished I could be alone. I soon would be, but not in a way that comforted me for long.

Even though we were practically living together at that point, I still had my own apartment. It was somewhere I could retreat whenever I needed to "work late" or whatever other excuse I'd offer for simply needing alone time. He dropped me off, and after a measly attempt at goodbye, I turned towards my door. I unlocked it, walked inside, and only turned around to watch him drive away when I knew he wouldn't be looking. The relationship ended soon after.

If I had entered that relationship as the person I am today, I'm sure it would've been great. Wedding bells, settling down, and all the typical signs of two people choosing each other. I realize now how hurtful my response must have been and how confusing it must have felt to be turned down and abandoned by someone so seemingly invested in the relationship. However, even though that moment was one of my worst relationship failures, it taught me the most.

After months of convincing myself we weren't meant to be together, I couldn't shake the guilt. I tried to believe that the feeling I got when he proposed was my intuition stopping me from making the biggest mistake of my life. But it wasn't until he moved on that my healing journey began. While he was getting engaged to someone new, I was wallowing at home in my apartment after my third breakup since we were together.

The proof that I might've been wrong was becoming painfully clear. I couldn't continue to ignore the common denominator in all my failed relationships – me.

A lot has changed in my life since.

After years of personal growth, research, and professional support, I've made progress that I assume many would say isn't possible for someone with an avoidant attachment style. Despite spending my life feeling dissatisfied in relationships, I've realized the value of them. I no longer feel the need to keep them distant or surface-level. Relationships are an integral part of my joy and well-being.

I'm so much more open than ever before in a way that truly feeds my soul. I've worked hard to lower my guard and stop running from connection. It feels so good to say I've gotten a second chance at profound love. I've chosen to fight through my avoidant impulses, and it's been magical. Now, I want nothing more than to help other avoidants have the same experiences.

This book is my chance to share what I've learned beyond the walls I used to put up. It's my chance to show you that although you may feel just fine on your own, you have the potential to feel incredible. There is nothing more valuable than love.

Before I knew anything about attachment styles, I looked for signs of insecurity in others without considering my own. I was always detaching and blaming. But healing starts with accepting the truth about avoidant attachment: We're not as secure as we may feel.

Throughout this book, I'll share the exact strategies I used to help me get where I am today. To heal, we must understand that our avoidant behavior does not come from a place of poor intent. We want love just as much as the next person. We may just be very good at giving up on it when things get real.

In this Chapter, I'll tell you the exact moment I decided to change. Although your story will be different from mine, I'll describe my transformation and successes, trusting that it will inspire you to embark on your own healing journey.

Remember, this isn't a journey towards changing who you are. It's a journey towards sticking around and experiencing the love you may (secretly) **really** want. It's about opening up in a way that feels liberating, reaching out in a way that feels exhilarating, and connecting to others in a way that makes you genuinely want to *stay.*

DEFINING LOVE: A TURNING POINT IN MY RELATIONSHIPS

I never thought I was the problem in any of my failed relationships. I found pride in having high standards and being a strong, independent partner who could enter relationships without baggage. But, oh boy, was my perception murky!

Whenever a relationship would end, I usually did the leaving. And when I left, my partners reacted in ways that ultimately confirmed my suspicions and beliefs about them. I believed they were insecure and had poor self-regulation skills, which often repulsed me. When they became emotional and overwhelmed, it felt easier to turn away and never look back. I wasn't aware that it was largely my behavior driving them crazy.

It was always a "them" problem and never a "me" problem.

But when I sat alone in my apartment and saw my ex's engagement post on social media, I had a very rude awakening. My stomach dropped, and all the negative internal dialogue I had built up about him dissolved. I saw him as the one who got away, and it hurt.

The level of anger I felt in that moment surpassed anything I'd ever felt. And it was all directed at me. My internal conflict went on for days and became a downward spiral. I fell into a deep depression. But I had no one else to blame. I couldn't escape the responsibility for a situation I created.

As a logical person, I didn't wallow for too long. I did the practical thing and booked an appointment with the nearest therapist. I didn't want to wait, and I didn't let anyone else in on what was happening. I believed my inner turmoil was a problem the therapist could fix for me.

Of course, having never been to therapy before, I had no idea what I was in for. My therapist had no intention of "fixing" anything. It was all up to me. The first appointment was tough, but it felt good to let someone in on my thoughts for a change. I both loved and hated it at the same time. However, the lightness I felt afterward was enough to encourage a second appointment, and then another, and another.

Getting professional feedback on things I'd locked away for years was a significant turning point in my life. And it was the start of something unexpected.

Before my appointment, I had little clue as to why I was depressed. Like going to the doctor with an illness, forgetting where I contracted it, I went in looking for answers. As luck would have it, my therapist had a very fitting specialization despite his general practice – relationships! He was the first to point out that the trigger for my depression was likely a relationship issue. We quickly got into the topic of attachment styles.

I soaked everything up like a sponge, and things soon made sense. I didn't reject my ex's proposal because of any fault in the relationship. It was the opposite. The relationship was too good for my avoidant nature. It scared the living daylight out of me.

Something about that realization made me incredibly sad. But it also sparked something new that I hadn't often experienced. It evoked a sense of compassion for myself as I realized my struggles were fear-related. I was scared, and there's very little you can do or say to invalidate fear. It's a powerful emotion. It seldom comes without reason.

Having acquired the right terminology to describe my experience in relationships, aka. Avoidantly Attached, I dove deeper into the topic of attachment theory. I read self-help books (keeping them hidden in my bedside drawer), engaged in online forums, and watched every video I could. And this was where things took a turn.

How Research Fueled My Healing Journey

What's interesting about the information available online is that there seems to be an oversaturation of negative content about avoidant attachment. If I wasn't careful, I'd find myself feeling rather battered and bruised. With countless comments like "They'll never change" or "Just leave, you're wasting your time." I felt as though these comments represented a challenge. One that I was determined to overcome.

I thought, "Oh, avoidants can't change? Watch me!"

It wasn't easy. It was extremely painful and, at times, damn near terrifying. After a lifetime of rigid rules, boundaries, and patterns, I had to push to expand my comfort zone. I won't say I didn't feel the urge to run when the lows came around—even some of the best times brought intense fear. But this is where the rewards of healing far outweigh the negatives. For example:

- **Moving in with my partner:** I had to finally let go of my apartment. I no longer had a "safe space" to retreat to when I wanted to escape. I had to learn to find safety and maintain a sense of autonomy within my relationship.

- **Saying "Yes!" to an engagement:** I had to overcome the fear of being "tied down" and let someone get closer to me than I believe anyone else has ever been.

- **Having children:** This one was possibly the most difficult to face as I always believed that motherhood meant the end of my autonomy. It wasn't true. Maybe for the first year, but with a loving partner to support me, my son has brought me nothing but joy.

While these were moments where I felt destined to mess up, they've become some of my most treasured. Even when my fear was urging me to shut down, push away, and detach emotionally, I kept going. And I honestly feel that I've proved my point. Avoidant attachment **can** heal. We can learn to love closeness, let others into our problems, and build successful, lasting relationships.

Despite the negative labels I've adorned over the years, including "cold-hearted," "narcissist," and "lone-wolf," the progress I've made on this journey has surpassed my expectations.

The Rewards Of Attachment: Secure Love

My current relationship has progressed far beyond any romantic relationship I've had. But hitting milestones is not an indication of health and fulfillment. What matters is the way a relationship feels. What matters is the depth of the connection.

I used to look down on couples that relied on each other. But that was before I experienced the rewards of secure love. I've learned a lot since pushing past my fears and building a far healthier relationship than ever before.

Secure love is warm and beautiful. It's a place where avoidant attachment can transform into openness and authenticity. It's fulfilling in a way that can't compare to the relationships we keep at a "comfortable" distance. It creates a space where we can continue to be ourselves while being fully appreciated by someone else.

However, secure love is not going to be comfortable at first. When relationships have always felt draining or cumbersome, we may find that we enter secure love slowly and with apprehension. That's okay.

While I will encourage you to push yourself to a healthy degree throughout this book, opening up too fast, too soon, will not help. We have to start at the beginning and slowly melt away our potentially harsh exterior to let others in without feeling like we're drowning.

CONCLUSION

My journey has been arduous. I've seen the end of too many otherwise good relationships and been left with hurtful labels that don't reflect my intentions. I've faced the intense guilt and self-loathing that comes from letting go of someone amazing – out of fear alone. But all of that has led me to do the therapy, research, and self-development to be a guiding light for you. All I can hope is that this book has found you sooner than this information found me.

I don't just believe that healing is possible. I *know* it is. If you're willing to see it as a challenge and move forward with curiosity, you can heal, too. You have the potential to build relationships that you genuinely want to be in, through thick and thin.

This chapter has been about my journey, but this book is about yours.

If you're ready to face the chaos of relationships and become a stronger, more secure person in love, turn the page, and let's begin. Chapter 2 will satisfy your avoidant fears, including what they are and where they came from. This is an important yet potentially painful step along this journey, but I assure you it'll be worth it.

You don't have to go it alone, either. The LearnWell Community can support you along the way.

2

UNDERSTANDING AVOIDANT ATTACHMENT

The Science Behind Our Fears

"Love is at the root of everything. All learning. All parenting. All relationships. Love, or the lack of it."

– Fred Rogers

WHAT AVOIDANT ATTACHMENT FEELS LIKE

Hollow. I felt lifeless in the face of intimacy. I'd be vibrant and engaging, only to drop out emotionally when I felt pressured to lean in and connect deeply. One loving look, another milestone, or a simple request for more was all it took for me to switch. I'd pull away. My emotions would twist, and negative thoughts would begin to smudge the positive memories we'd built.

"This is too much. I need space."

"Why do they always do this? Isn't the way things are enough?"

"I'm ruining this. But it's for the best. They aren't right for me."

When my avoidance triggered, it felt as though my "real" feelings were waking up. It was as if all the wonderful feelings I'd experienced before were an illusion, seen through rose-colored glasses. My thoughts would spiral when alone, and I'd allow them to slowly transform my partner into the person I feared them to be. Suddenly, they were needy, too much, and oversensitive. I'd feel smothered and leave.

I became so good at leaving relationships that I'd feel guilty for my cold, matter-of-fact approach to breakups. I'd feel so certain about ending things even though I knew how much my partner cared for me.

Next, I'd recoil back to my comfort zone – somewhere I could be alone. My shoulders would ease, and I could "think clearly" without all the pressure. Then, things would go one of two ways:

1. I'd leave my partner and reject contact – sometimes forever.

2. Or, I'd leave my partner only to realize I was wrong, too late.

The first outcome always felt best for me. I no longer cared about the relationship enough to worry about them moving on. I truly believed that ending things was best for both of us, even though my belief wasn't based on much evidence.

Outcome two was one I never expected. I always trusted my own judgment and went with my feelings about the partner and the relationship. Usually, these feelings would last and I'd continue to feel certain about my choice to break up. But when my negative feelings would dissolve and I'd become flooded with good memories, including all the love and pain they'd bring, regret was the natural consequence.

Even though I can now see a clear pattern in my thoughts, emotions, behaviors, and fears, I didn't have the self-awareness to realize it back then. Only now that I've done the work to observe my behavior and analyze my relationship history can I look back and see my poor judgment.

Avoidant attachment can make us believe that relationships are unsafe and that solitude is the only solution.[1] It can make us see others as a threat to our success as they become reliant on us – even in healthy ways. The minute we perceive someone becoming reliant on us, clinging to us, or needing us in a way that feels like a burden, our avoidant impulses surface. We may experience a rush of thoughts and feelings that make us want to detach, defend ourselves, and disconnect.

In this chapter, we'll cover the scientific explanation of avoidant attachment, the harmful beliefs we may have acquired in childhood, and the chemical differences impacting our well-being. Then, I'll introduce you to your experiential framework for healing: The Wall Of Detachment. This is where you get answers about why you may be avoidant and how avoidant attachment holds you back.

THE SCIENCE BEHIND AVOIDANCE IN RELATIONSHIPS

Our attachment style starts forming in infancy and develops throughout childhood based on our relationship with primary caregivers.[2] It is the way we learn to form, enjoy, and maintain relationships that are important to us. In an ideal world, we would form a secure attachment style, which is characterized by:[3]

- Feeling comfortable forming close relationships.

- Healthy communication skills and conflict resolution.

- Having a high self-esteem and a secure sense of self.

- Good emotional management and communication.

However, if we experience trauma, dysfunction, or other disturbances of healthy attachment formation, we can form an insecure attachment style. These include:

- Avoidant Attachment: Generally characterized by avoidant behavior in relationships with predominantly positive feelings about ourselves and negative feelings about others.[4] Includes an instinct to protect one's sense of self through distance.

- Anxious Attachment: Generally characterized by anxious behavior in relationships with predominantly positive feelings about others and negative feelings about ourselves.[5] Includes an instinct to protect one's sense of self through closeness.

- Disorganized Attachment: Generally characterized by both avoidant and anxious behavior with predominantly negative feelings about ourselves and others. Includes a disorganized alternation between protecting one's sense of self through closeness and distance.

It's important to note that attachment styles have some fluidity. They can not only shift depending on the relationships we're in, but they can improve.[6] We can heal. That's why you're here, because it's possible. This book is my testimony. Even if you don't relate to every aspect of avoidant attachment in every relationship, keep reading. There are tools here that can help you.

Avoidant attachment, also known as dismissive avoidant attachment, is not about heartlessly shuffling through relationships, escaping when our cup is full. It's a defense mechanism built into our nervous system to protect us from rejection, criticism, and other fears.[7] Although we may not have adequate information about how we were parented as babies, our childhoods can hold enough clues to help us understand where our avoidant attachment came from. Let's use my story as an example.

My dad wasn't around, so I won't say much about him. All that matters is that he abandoned us when I was a baby and disappeared. Of course, that played a role in how my attachment style formed, but my mom had more of an impact because she was present. She's amazing. I love her more than anything. But being a single mother took its toll.

I spent much time alone as a child, even though I had many friends. My mother worked full-time as a waitress, and when I was old enough, I'd walk myself home from school. This wasn't such a bad thing. I had neighbors who would take me in and let me do my homework in front of their TV. However, when I had a problem, I don't remember ever talking to my mom about it. I'd either ask my friends for advice or figure it out on my own.

My whole childhood felt like something I figured out on my own.

When my mom and I spent time together, we kept things fairly surface-level and light. She was so burnt out from work that all she had the energy for was a simple microwave dinner or takeout and a comedy movie on the sofa. We'd sit and laugh, enjoying our dinners, even when I could feel something wasn't right.

My mom didn't respond well to my mood changes. Whether I cried over a bully at school or confronted her about working late all the time, she got overwhelmed easily and would lock herself in her room to avoid the discussions. I quickly learned that my feelings only made things worse. I began to put on a happy mask the minute I heard her key turn at the front door after work.

As I grew older, I remember crying in my room a lot. Feeling upset, I'd lock myself in – like my mom did. I had a lot of anger that I didn't always know how to cope with. But I'd eventually calm myself down, or rather, distract myself out of it. It was only when I got into fights with my friends and later on in romantic relationships that I realized not everyone prefers coping alone.

From a very young age, I learned to cope with life and its challenges with little emotional support. My childhood was the perfect environment for self-reliance, a fear of rejection, and a deep aversion to feeling my feelings. That's why I formed an avoidant attachment.

As we continue, reflect on the following points and be prepared to pinpoint the parts of your childhood that may have contributed to your attachment style. For avoidant attachment to form, primary caregivers would have had to instill one or more of the following beliefs in their child:

- **Relationships are not safe places to be vulnerable.** For example, a parent who yells or becomes frustrated when their child opens up to them.

- **Opening up about negative feelings will lead to rejection.** For example, a parent who praises positive emotions and responds negatively to negative emotions.

- **Intimacy lets people get closer to you, which may lead to rejection.** For example, a parent who would distance themselves after a short period of closeness.

- **Dependency on others is a sign of weakness. Self-sufficiency makes you strong.** For example, a parent who models extreme independence and holds these beliefs themselves.

- **Trust is dangerous and can lead to disappointment and betrayal.** For example, a parent who breaks promises, doesn't stick to their word, and lies to their child.

- **My needs are not important; other people's needs should always come first.** For example, a parent who is self-sacrificing and hard-working despite the negative impact on them and their children.

- **Love is conditional and is based on performance and behavior.** For example, a parent who only responds positively to their child when their child is getting straight A's or winning their soccer matches.

Many parenting styles and childhood circumstances can lead to avoidant attachment. This experience is impactful because it influences our beliefs about ourselves and our relationships.

I've put together a simple exercise in your Workbook where you can note which aspects of your childhood may have contributed to your attachment style. Take a moment to complete it now, I know it will help validate some of your childhood wounds. When you're done, return to me for the science of avoidant attachment.

The Chemical Rollercoaster Of Avoidance

Good relationships hold value that can't be fulfilled elsewhere. They impact our nervous systems in unique ways that signal safety and boost the "feel-good" brain chemicals responsible for feeling loved, connected, and happy, including:[8]

- **Oxytocin:** This is the love hormone, responsible for feelings of love, warmth, and closeness with someone else.[9] In avoidant attachment, we may be deficient in oxytocin because we seldom let others close enough to allow for oxytocin release. For example, during long hugs, intimate touch, or cuddling.

- **GABA:** Without enough oxytocin, we inhibit the activation of a neurotransmitter called GABA.[10] This neurotransmitter signals important neural chemistry that impacts sleep, cortisol levels, and available magnesium.[11] As avoidant attachers, we may notice that we struggle with chronic sleep issues, high cortisol levels, and tight muscles.

- **Vasopressin:** Vasopressin creates the emotional bond we feel when solving problems with someone and is responsible for the protectiveness we may feel over someone we love, particularly in males.[12] In avoidant attachment, we may prefer to solve problems on our own robbing us of opportunities to feel connected with others, because we may not see others as capable or trustworthy enough to solve problems efficiently.

- **Serotonin:** Often dubbed the "happy hormone" healthy serotonin levels can create lasting feelings of improved well-being and happiness.[13] Although there are many ways to increase serotonin levels, positive social experiences are a profound resource that is easy to access once we've built healthy relationships.

- **Dopamine:** Responsible for feelings of motivation and reward, dopamine is a powerful and addictive chemical. However, unlike the other "feel-good" chemicals, we tend to use dopamine as a lifeline that keeps us functioning. It's one of the easiest brain chemicals we can produce completely alone through activities that activate our reward center like eating junk food, online shopping, or playing video games.[14]

When we have an avoidant attachment, we may have spent a lifetime deficient in the experiences that produce these important chemicals. This may cause us to function without them in a way that may make us believe we don't need them. However, the truth is we do. Without good, lasting relationships, we're leaving a vital resource for joy untapped.

Without healthy relationships to offer us connection, love, and a sense of safety, we may constantly be chasing something without knowing what it is. We may feel hollow without understanding how fulfilling a deep connection can be. Or, we may know exactly what we need but feel too scared to go after it and allow it to sustain.

Avoidant attachment can place us on a chemical rollercoaster we struggle to get off. As we indulge in positive relationships, our "feel-good" chemicals increase only for our avoidant beliefs and impulses to become triggered by the closeness. Then, when we suddenly pull away and emotionally detach, those feel-good chemicals dissipate without positive input. Soon, we may feel empty and disconnected, using things like exercise, food, or other dopamine-boosting coping mechanisms to try and feel good again outside of the relationship. Those of us who are work-orientated may become increasingly busy during these times.

(Formatting: A graphic showing 3 outcomes: 1. How relationships offer a positive influx of feel-good chemicals, 2. how being alone too long reduces those chemicals, and 3. how our lonely attempts to fill up on feel-good chemicals doesn't satisfy us. For example:

Connection Fuels Feel-Good Chemicals

No Input = Feel-Good Chemicals Plummet

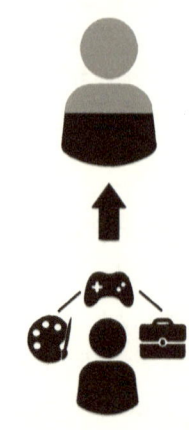
Dopamine-Fueled Feel-Good Chemicals Don't Fulfill Us

This is not a sustainable way to be happy. Dopamine will always be fleeting, and the easiest ways to get it are often the least healthy. Healthy relationships are essential for feeling fulfilled, even if they're only good friendships.

Understanding the brain chemistry behind our avoidant tendencies helps us realize just how visceral our experience can be. It's not just in our heads but in our bodies. However, it doesn't give us the tools to change them. Becoming more secure is not as simple as forcing ourselves into relationships for a steady supply of oxytocin.

This is where I'd like to introduce you to The Wall Of Detachment—the model that will carry you through this healing journey. It will help you learn what can happen when your avoidance is triggered so you can improve your relationship patterns and gently expand your comfort zone. Relationships can feel good, engaging, and worth the trouble. Let me show you how.

THE WALL OF DETACHMENT: 5 WAYS WE BLOCK PEOPLE OUT TO KEEP OURSELVES SAFE

As I mentioned in Chapter 1, avoidant attachment is a fear issue, even if we don't want to believe it is. It's recognized as an insecure attachment style because, on some level, we experience insecurity in relationships.

Our childhood experiences, and sometimes the relationships we experience later in life, may have taught us that relationships aren't safe places to get our needs met.[15] We may even believe they aren't safe to be in at all.

With our fear steering the ship, we put up a wall. We pull away, shut others out, and can even stay guarded when things feel good. I call this The Wall Of Detachment, built with 5 vital layers, including thoughts, emotions, behaviors, and two major fears: vulnerability and intimacy. Take a look at this diagram before we dive deeper into each layer:

The Wall Of Detachment

- Detached Mindset
- Defensive Emotions
- Deactivating Behaviors
- Doubtful Vulnerability
- Distant Intimacy

The Wall Of Detachment is our defense mechanism. We put it up each time our avoidant attachment is triggered. When we are in a relationship, this mechanism may be activated most of the time, especially if the relationship is already unhealthy. We will discuss triggers throughout Part 2, including how to recognize them. This will be important as we break down the Wall. But, for now, let's look at each layer.

Detached Mindset

Think back to the list of harmful beliefs that our caregivers may have instilled in us. These beliefs accumulate to form our mindset about relationships. When we believe things like "Relationships are not safe places to be vulnerable" and "Dependency on others is a sign of weakness," we may form a mindset that favors detachment.

A detached mindset is dangerous because it catalyzes the other layers in The Wall Of Detachment. It includes a host of negative thoughts that keep our guard up, including:

- "I don't need anyone, I can handle everything on my own."
- "I need to keep this to myself. Emotions are a sign of weakness."
- "Relationships are more trouble than they're worth."
- "People always end up needing too much from me."
- "If I show them the real me, they wouldn't see me the same."

- "I'm comfortable with the way things are. Why would I ruin this with marriage, moving in, etc.?"

- "They only love me for what I can offer. They don't love the real me."

- "We've had a great time, but now that they want more, I can see we aren't compatible."

Because these thoughts can feel ingrained in us, we may be reluctant to change them or fail to see why they're so bad. A detached mindset can create unhealthy thinking patterns, which we will discuss in Chapter 3. Most importantly, it can lead to defensive emotions.

Defensive Emotions

The foundation of avoidant attachment is a need to protect ourselves from uncomfortable emotions and others' instability.[16] A significant portion of that protection is how we experience, process, and express our emotions. We tend to handle emotions defensively to protect ourselves from the pain while we soldier on through tough relationship outcomes.

We may choose to suppress rather than express emotions.

In avoidant attachment, we may also suppress certain positive emotions if we believe they make us appear soft. For example:

- Reducing the way we express joy to appear more neutral about a situation.

- Avoiding situations where we may be expected to express ourselves emotionally, like giving a wedding speech or even going on a date somewhere private and quiet.

- Opting out of activities that may bring our guards down like family game nights, where we may fear that our goofy side slips through.

Defensive emotions diminish our joy and prevent us from expressing our needs appropriately. However, we may not always intentionally keep others in the dark about our feelings. Often, we may have suppressed our emotions for so long that we no longer feel or understand them accurately.

This lack of understanding, paired with a failure to express ourselves, can lead to behaviors that help us avoid or escape otherwise healthy relationships.

Deactivating Behaviors

Imagine a situation where your partner wants to support you through a problem. They want to help, but all you can think is, "I can handle this on my own." You start feeling frustrated, and it doesn't make sense to your partner. Then, you experience an impulse to be alone and follow through by leaving the room. You've missed an opportunity to bond with your partner, and the next time you see them, you pretend nothing happened to avoid conflict.

This is how The Wall Of Detachment reinforces behaviors that keep us deactivated.

Deactivating behaviors, clinically known as deactivating strategies, often follow an avoidant impulse.[17] They are reinforced by our defensive emotions and detached mindset, which only keep us committed to our behavioral choices. Also, they are not active behaviors. Deactivating behaviors are generally passive, reductive, or escapist. They can include:

- Walking away from arguments or trying to avoid them.
- Shutting down during conflict and refusing to speak or make contact.
- Ignoring problems, hoping they will go away without addressing them.
- Working too much in an attempt to keep a relationship from progressing too quickly.
- Delaying long-term commitment even when we want the relationship to progress.
- Avoiding emotional and physical intimacy to reduce the chances of dependency.
- Fixating on others' mistakes or flaws to justify keeping an emotional distance.
- Prioritizing hobbies, friends, or other personal interests to maintain a sense of independence even if it causes us to neglect the relationship.
- Making excuses like "I'm too busy", "We're just not compatible", or "I don't want a relationship" to stay comfortably disconnected.

Deactivating behaviors may reinforce our greatest relationship challenges because they keep us in our comfort zone. They keep us from opening up, being vulnerable, or engaging intimately with others.

Doubtful Vulnerability & Distant Intimacy

The final layers involve two major fears in avoidant attachment: Vulnerability and intimacy. They form part of the wall because our detached mindset, defensive emotions, and deactivating behaviors may interfere with how we experience them. Both vulnerability and intimacy are essential elements of healthy relationships.

As avoidant attachers, we may still engage in both. However, when our wall goes up, we may doubt the positive impact of our vulnerability and prefer to refrain from it where possible. We may lack the trust necessary to open up authentically, keeping our displays of vulnerability surface-level.

We each have our limits when it comes to intimacy. However, with intimate acts like dates, physical touch, or deep conversations, we will likely maintain an emotional distance that is almost palpable. We may go on dates without getting close, engage in physical intimacy with little emotional availability, and keep deep conversations one-sided.

There are many ways to be intimate without fully committing ourselves to it. We may use intimacy to maintain our relationships just enough to keep them going without allowing the connection to progress.

Vulnerability and intimacy are two of the most important aspects of a fulfilling relationship. Without them, we can never gain the closeness necessary for authentic, long-lasting connections.

To break down The Wall Of Detachment, we need to work slowly. Taking a sledgehammer to our protective wall will only leave us exposed and pushed to our limits or beyond. However, we must break down this wall to feel the freedom and lightness of a secure attachment. If we gently let our walls crumble, layer by layer, we will have time to adjust and feel refreshed by growth.

CONCLUSION

Our struggles are not without reason. They come from a lifetime of reinforced beliefs, emotions, behaviors, and fears. They are taught to us by caregivers who model the level of safety and reliability we can expect in relationships. They influence our brain chemistry, which can keep us on a rollercoaster of well-being. Soon, they build into a wall.

The Wall Of Detachment is an essential framework encompassing 5 layers of avoidant attachment. It includes:

- Detached mindset
- Defensive emotions
- Deactivating behaviors
- Doubtful vulnerability
- Distant intimacy

This is the wall we put up when we feel at risk of getting hurt, let down, or robbed of our independence. Whenever a situation triggers our avoidant attachment, the wall goes up and we shut others out in various ways. But I have a solution. One I've practiced with rewards far outweighing any risk.

I'm not asking you to tear down your walls within a week. I'm proposing you turn the page and begin a steady deconstruction, one layer at a time.

This is the end of Part 1 and the beginning of all the practical steps available to you. Throughout Part 2, I will offer one simple step per chapter to effectively address and dissolve each layer so you can learn to let others in and safely become more engaged, connected, and fulfilled.

PART 2

DISMANTLING THE WALL OF DETACHMENT: FROM DISCONNECTED TO ENGAGED, OPEN, AND PRESENT

3

A DETACHED MINDSET: REWIRING MY AVOIDANT BRAIN

How I Used Neuroplasticity To Create Secure Love

"To be capable of steady friendship or lasting love, are the two greatest proofs, not only of goodness of heart, but of strength of mind."

– William Hazlitt

ADDRESSING THE FIRST LAYER OF THE WALL OF DETACHMENT

Like a dark cloud, thoughts about the argument hung over me. They followed me to work, lingered during my drive home, and kept me awake that night. Normally, I could move on within a few minutes of being alone. But it was the first time a partner ever confronted my avoidance directly. With piercing eyes, he said, "You're not even really here, are you?"

I felt exposed. It was as if he could see right through me. I kept my emotions aloof and my reactions minimal to stay detached and in control. But at that moment, he tore my guard down, and I cried. My tears attracted the response I was avoiding. His empathy felt like pity. It took me a week to get my mind straight again.

With my detached mindset still front and center, I did the only thing I believed I could do. I left. The idea of staying with someone who made me feel vulnerable was unnerving. Leaving was the only solution I could muster.

The trouble with leaving a person who could see behind my wall—my personal Wall Of Detachment—was that without them, there was no one to question my thoughts or behavior. I could justify my avoidance, validate my limiting thoughts, and carry on living with my guard up. I could stay comfortable and neglect my personal growth.

My detached mindset kept me stuck. I didn't allow anyone else to enter my life and shake things up. I didn't think that was valuable because I didn't realize there was anything wrong with the way I was. That was until I found myself perpetually alone, disconnected, and unhappy. With no one to blame and no one around to push my buttons, I had to do something that felt incredibly unnatural to me. I had to question myself.

With the help of my growing interest in improving my life, I started to analyze my thoughts. As valid as they felt, my thoughts maintained a familiar pattern. They were:

- **Judgmental:** I used others' flaws and mistakes to help justify my impulse to detach and escape. I judged people for being emotional, prioritizing their relationships, and valuing things like marriage or holding hands in public.

- **Limiting:** My beliefs about relationships and what constitutes a successful person were very limiting, sometimes even harmful. I had an incredibly narrow view of what behaviors were acceptable in others and held people to impossibly high standards. For example, I believed that needing a partner would make me weak, that expressing negative emotions directly was bad manners, and that conflict was a sign that a relationship was destined to fail.

- **Distorted:** I was subject to many distorted thinking patterns, also known as cognitive distortions, which only confused my true thoughts and feelings. Your workbook includes a list of cognitive distortions for your reference. For example, my thoughts often followed an "all-or-nothing" pattern. This manifested as high expectations in relationships and very quick and definite reactions when those expectations were not met. I'd also like to encourage you to share which distorted thinking patterns concern you most in the LearnWell Community.

In the previous chapter, I listed a few common negative thoughts we may experience in avoidant attachment. We spoke about how these thoughts indicate a detached mindset. Avoidant attachment can cause thinking patterns, beliefs, and a mindset that misleads us in relationships.

A detached mindset is focused on developing negative expectations of others while maintaining a higher rating of ourselves.[18] This is not our fault. It happens because of the attachment style we naturally formed due to our childhood circumstances and relationships. But that doesn't mean we can't grow.

The moment I switched my focus onto authentic growth to improve my mindset was the moment my relationships shifted. I no longer felt so alone; I started realizing the value of connection and allowed more joy into my life. In the introduction of this book, I listed 5 steps I will offer you throughout Part 2 to counteract the 5 layers in The Wall Of Detachment. In this chapter, I'm going to share Step 1. I'll encourage you to build a secure mindset using well-founded psychological techniques.

STEP 1: BUILD A SECURE MINDSET

Dissolving our detached mindset and gradually building it into a secure mindset is the first step to breaking down The Wall Of Detachment and nurturing an earned secure attachment. It will help us foster a more secure dynamic in relationships. We will no longer believe that we must shut others out and can comfortably continue this journey.

A secure mindset is balanced. It allows us to see both ourselves and others from a more realistic point of view. With a secure mindset, we can validate our experience while questioning whether it is aligned with truth. We may see the flaws in our judgment more easily and feel willing to adjust our thinking.

Having a secure mindset is not about being flawless and always thinking positively. Security lies in the way we handle our mistakes. Once we have built a secure mindset, we may still judge others, hold some limiting beliefs, and experience negative thinking patterns. We're human. To strive for security in ourselves and our relationships, we only need to strive for the awareness required to better manage our thoughts, emotions, behaviors, and fears.

There are various well-studied practices for building a greater awareness of our thoughts and, therefore, a more secure mindset. Each of these practices uses the principles of neuroplasticity, a theory explaining how the brain is malleable and can be rewired to let go of harmful thinking patterns to adopt new thoughts, beliefs, and mindsets.[19]

These 3 brain-rewiring techniques will help you improve your thoughts now and in the long term. The more you practice them, the more you can mold your mindset into something that expands your life. Remember, a detached mindset consists of avoidant thoughts and harmful beliefs. We can build a secure mindset by adopting more secure beliefs and thinking more securely.

Technique 1: Manage Avoidant Thoughts With Mindfulness

Mindfulness is a practice with benefits ranging from improved physical health to increased relationship satisfaction.[20] It's based on the principle of grounding one's attention into the present moment and becoming more in tune with our bodily sensations, thoughts, and environment. Practicing mindfulness regularly can cause long-lasting effects that physiologically change our brains for the better.[21]

One particularly helpful benefit of a mindfulness practice is its impact on attention. By increasing activation in the areas of our brain responsible for attention, mindfulness can help us process information more realistically.[22] This can mean improving the accuracy of our judgment. It can help us determine which thoughts are based on fears and which impulses are healthy responses.

For example, when I started taking time to breathe and tune my awareness to my thoughts, bodily sensations, and immediate environment, I became more able to see my avoidant impulses for what they were: fear. I'd feel my stomach tense under my partner's gaze. My mind would fill with thoughts like, "This feels uncomfortable, but I don't know why. Maybe they're not right for me." and I'd experience a sudden urge to leave, push them away, or withdraw. That awareness gave me the ability to rethink how I wanted to respond. I was no longer at the whim of my avoidant impulses.

Practicing mindfulness is a simple way to gain awareness of our thoughts and emotions. We'll discuss emotions in Chapter 4, including why we may not experience them as intensely as those around us. But for now, know that the work you do here will ripple down The Wall Of Detachment.

For an effective mindfulness practice, take 5 minutes every day to complete these steps:

1. Breathe

Pause whatever you are doing and take a couple of deep breaths. This will help you slow down and bring your awareness into a more relaxed and reflective state.

2. Acknowledge Thoughts And Sensations

Bring your awareness to your thoughts and any bodily sensations. Without acting on them, acknowledge them, no matter how subtle or strange they may be. For example, you may notice thoughts like:

- "Why am I doing this?"
- "This is pointless."
- "I wonder how long I'll keep this up."

Whatever thoughts come up for you, simply allow them to appear and disappear without judgment or interference. The same goes for sensations. You may experience:

- Urges to stop the practice, leave the situation, withdraw, or self-soothe.
- Physical symptoms of emotions such as an increased heart rate or a knot in your stomach.

3. Question Your Experience

In avoidant attachment, we may rarely question ourselves while constantly questioning others. It may be difficult to believe or admit that our experience doesn't always reflect the whole truth. To form a secure mindset, we have to balance things out by learning to discern our own experience.

Question your experience with a sense of curiosity. This isn't about invalidating thoughts or feelings but rather gaining clarity. Ask questions like:

- Why do I feel this why?
- Where are these thoughts coming from?
- What is my body trying to tell me?
- What am I trying to accomplish by detaching right now?
- How can I respond in a healthier way for myself and others?

Mindfulness doesn't always mean doing something to change the experience. Simply being aware of the experience is powerful enough. Taking 5 minutes to practice mindfulness, regardless of when or why we're practicing, can slowly train our brains to be more self-aware. In your Workbook, I've included a 7-day challenge to help you make mindfulness a habit. This will be important as we continue deconstructing The Wall Of Detachment.

Avoidant attachment can cause significant detachment from our own thoughts and emotions.[23] But mindfulness helps to strengthen our judgment and add more nuance to our understanding. Once we gain an awareness of our thoughts, we are in the perfect position to apply the next technique.

Technique 2: Transform Negative Thoughts With Cognitive Restructuring

For most of my life, I was at the whim of every thought I experienced. I had no control and felt like I had to act on every impulse, even if it meant destroying a good relationship. I held my thoughts and impulses in high regard and didn't realize they could work against me. But when I learned about cognitive distortions and how far our minds can go to distort reality, I realized that my thoughts don't always reflect truth.

Neuroplasticity is all about neural pathways in the brain and how we can actively improve our own "wiring" with new thoughts and behaviors. Quite literally, we can change our brains to *be* more secure just by choosing to think more secure thoughts. This is where cognitive restructuring is key.

Cognitive restructuring is a technique proven to gently shift negative thinking for the long term by consciously changing our thoughts.[24] It gives us control over our thoughts in a way that can help us replace false beliefs and build a more secure mindset.[25]

Over time, this exercise can reveal thought patterns you can expect to experience again. As you practice, make a mental note of the patterns you discover. Be ready to remind yourself of what you've learned when these thought patterns resurface so you can mindfully manage them. Soon, it will be easier to discern which thoughts and emotions are based on past difficulties or avoidant attachment and which ones are valid for the present circumstance.

To practice cognitive restructuring:[26]

1. Identify A Negative Thought

In avoidant attachment, you might not notice a negative thought right away. Instead, you may feel an urge to put up your wall or leave a situation. When you feel an avoidant impulse like this, stop, take a deep breath, and bring your awareness to your thoughts. Notice what thoughts come up with the impulse. Identify the most prominent thought or negative thinking pattern.

For example, when I experience an urge to withdraw during conversation, I might think, "This is getting too intense." This is an example of emotional reasoning, one of the cognitive distortions you will have seen in your Workbook.

2. Consider The Evidence

Once you've identified the negative thought or thinking pattern, consider the evidence of the situation. Ask questions to gain clarity about the validity of the thought. For example:

- What evidence do I have that supports or contradicts this thought?
- Is this thought based on facts or driven by emotions or assumptions?
- How might I view this situation if I were more objective?
- Is this thought influenced by past negative experiences?
- What evidence do I have to assume this person is a threat?

In my example, let's assume the conversation was calm and headed in a positive direction. I can then realize that the thought, "This is getting too intense," had little evidence to support it other than my subjective feelings of overwhelm.

However, if the person I'm with is irritated, I may acknowledge that the intensity I feel is valid but that my overwhelm may be influenced by past traumas. For example, if irritation led to abuse in my childhood, I can acknowledge the role trauma is playing. I can consider the evidence and realize that this person has only ever responded lovingly, even when they feel irritated. It is vital to keep evidence collection relevant to the current relationship.

3. Choose A New Thought

With the negative thought in mind, choose a new thought that reflects a more secure mindset. This can take the form of positive internal dialogue. For example:

- That thought isn't true. The truth is X.
- I'm only thinking X because of Y. I'd rather think Z.

In my example, I might change my thought from "This is getting too intense." to "I'm feeling overwhelmed by the level of closeness. But this is good for the relationship. I can handle this." In your Workbook, this exercise is laid out for you to try on a recent negative thought or thought pattern you've experienced.

Practicing cognitive restructuring is an important step. With time, the process can become automatic until transforming your thoughts becomes instinct. With more mindfulness about your thoughts and the ability to change them, the next technique will help you address false beliefs.

Technique 3: Address Harmful Beliefs With CBT

In avoidant attachment, we form harmful beliefs about relationships and other people. These can lead to negative thinking patterns, destructive behavioral impulses, and a detached mindset. However, with cognitive behavioral therapy (CBT), we can address them and reduce their impact. I've included a list of common harmful beliefs in your Workbook to help you with this technique.[27]

Cognitive behavioral therapy, or CBT, is one of the most widely practiced and studied forms of psychotherapy.[28] It is based on the idea that our thinking patterns and behaviors are learned, meaning they can be unlearned and replaced by new, more beneficial thinking patterns and behaviors.[29] We can use CBT to address and shift harmful beliefs by:[30]

1. Practicing Self-Compassion

In avoidant attachment, we may forget that we deserve kindness from ourselves. We may manage ourselves with an iron fist inside our minds. Our inner critic is often built on the hurtful words we heard growing up or in abusive relationships.[31] However, a harsh internal dialogue will only keep harmful beliefs ruminating.

Part of forming a secure mindset is learning to speak to ourselves compassionately. We must show ourselves the kind of care and understanding we'd offer a close friend. As you shift your beliefs, practice using a more compassionate internal dialogue. For example, you might change:

- "Why do I always do this?" to "This is a pattern. Now that I see it, let me see how I can improve."

- "I've got to keep this up or else I'm a failure." to "I'm doing the best I can, but it's okay to rest. My needs matter."

- "I shouldn't have been so weak" to "Expressing emotions is healthy. Showing my fear doesn't make me weak."

As you continue this exercise, you may face harmful beliefs you've carried for a lifetime. That's why it's important to use self-compassion to address those beliefs gently. It might feel strange at first, but we must learn to soothe ourselves in healthier ways. If it doesn't feel good when others talk down to us, we shouldn't talk down to ourselves.

However, self-compassion might feel strange at first. This is normal. Our negative thought patterns can be so ingrained that kindness feels uncomfortable. With time, you will start to notice the softness and ease that comes after speaking to yourself so kindly. This is a gentle rewriting of our internal narrative. Tackle it with a sense of curiosity. And if kindness is too confronting, aim for neutrality.

2. Explore Your Values

Values are a great indicator of beliefs. If we aren't sure of our beliefs, we can start by asking ourselves what we value in life and relationships. In your Workbook, follow the exercise that will guide you through this process so you can identify your harmful beliefs. For example, common things we may value in avoidant attachment and the harmful beliefs they may result in include:

- Self-sufficiency: "If I need help, it means I'm not capable enough."

- Independence: "I must rely on myself. Depending on others is a sign of weakness."

- Privacy: "Letting others in on my thoughts or feelings will give them power over me."

- Emotional self-control: "Expressing my emotions leaves me vulnerable to rejection."

- Competence: "If I'm not perfect or highly competent, I won't be valued or respected."

- Strength: "Vulnerability is a sign of weakness; I must always appear strong and unaffected."

These values are not negative. However, when we are avoidantly attached, we may hold ourselves to them in unhealthy ways, building harmful beliefs that damage our relationships. We can maintain the same values while forming new, healthier beliefs.

3. Form New Beliefs

Cognitive restructuring is a CBT technique used to choose new thoughts. But it can work just as well to form new beliefs. Now that you have a list of values you aspire to uphold, consider how you might form healthy beliefs around them. For example:

- Self-sufficiency: "Being capable makes me feel proud, and accepting help when I need it shows wisdom, not weakness."

- Independence: "Independence is important, and so is connection. I can rely on myself and still trust others without reducing my autonomy."

- Privacy: "Sharing my thoughts and feelings with trusted people is a way of building connection and understanding."

- Emotional self-control: "Expressing my emotions in healthy ways is a sign of strength and authenticity."

- Competence: "My worth isn't tied to perfection. I am valued and respected for who I am, not just for what I achieve."

- Strength: "True strength lies in being honest with myself and others. Vulnerability takes courage."

You can complete this exercise in your Workbook to solidify what you've learned and move on from this chapter with something tangible that will help shift your mindset each time you refer back to it. Being clear on your values and forming healthy beliefs around them is a phenomenal step towards security.[32]

With more awareness and control over your thoughts and beliefs, you can continue applying these 3 brain re-wiring techniques to build a more secure mindset. A secure mindset will take time and practice, but that doesn't mean we can't move on in the meantime.

As you continue this journey, you will have many more opportunities to practice secure thinking. Just as The Wall Of Detachment builds into a defensive mechanism, the steps throughout Part 2 will build into one holistic solution. Keep going, even if your mindset is still a work in progress.

CONCLUSION

A detached mindset limits us to the emotions, behaviors, and fears that exacerbate our avoidant attachment. It's the first layer in The Wall Of Detachment because when we address it, we gain the mental fortitude to embark on this journey with more security.

Once we shift our beliefs and improve our thoughts, we become empowered to face the following layers with compassion and clarity about our destination. To build a more secure mindset, we can actively:

- Practice mindfulness to become more present and aware of our thoughts.

- Use cognitive restructuring to identify and change negative thinking patterns.

- Apply CBT techniques to address and transform harmful beliefs.

Together, these 3 techniques give us the tools to break down our detached mindset so we can effectively build a new, more secure mindset that leads to secure emotions, behaviors, and safety in relationships.

However, although building a secure mindset will ripple down The Wall Of Detachment, it's not enough to see a sustainable change.

Each step you learn throughout Part 2 is necessary. Without the solutions they offer, you might find yourself repeating old patterns despite your improved thinking. We also can't completely claim a secure mindset when our emotions and behaviors are still avoidant, and our fears reign our truth. If you're ready to learn Step 2, deconstruct the next layer, and begin *feeling* the difference, turn the page.

4

DISMISSIVE EMOTIONS: LEARNING TO SPEAK 'EMOTION'

A Former Avoidants Guide

"Emotions can get in the way or get you on the way."
– Mavis Mazhura

UNDERSTANDING OUR OWN EMOTIONS TO UNDERSTAND OTHERS

I've always cared about my partners. I'd worry about their happiness, consider their feelings, and feel a sense of love and appreciation for them when things were going well. But something changed when things went wrong. And I didn't understand it until recently.

The minute the relationship became stressful, I'd go cold. I could feel my facial expression neutralize as my body drained of all emotion. It wasn't always instant. I'd feel angry and defensive, trying to participate in arguments I'd find myself in. But as the arguments swirled in a seemingly endless cycle of misunderstandings, it was as if someone flipped a switch inside me. Suddenly, I'd go numb. I couldn't argue, would barely move, and certainly didn't care anymore.

I started to feel like I really was "heartless."

Now that I know about attachment styles and have researched enough to understand my own, things make more sense. People with an avoidant attachment style have been shown to experience higher levels of alexithymia (uh-lek-suh-thai-mee-uh).[33] Alexithymia is a neuropsychological phenomenon impacting our ability to experience, identify, and express emotions.[34]

This means our nervous system may have developed a lack of sensitivity to emotions. It's not our fault that we detach or turn cold.[35] Our experiences in relationships have trained our nervous system to operate primarily in the fight-flight-or-freeze response in the face of stress.[36] In avoidant attachment, this can look like carelessness, stonewalling (which we will discuss in Chapter 5), and a lack of empathy.

However, it's not that we don't care about others; it's only that our nervous systems are not fully equipped to manage emotions securely. Each of us will experience alexithymia in unique ways and to varying degrees. We may:

- Experience emotional symptoms without being able to identify the emotion.

- Struggle to differentiate between emotional symptoms and physical sensations.

- Have trouble empathizing with others, when both feeling and showing empathy.[37]

- Avoid emotional situations as they may be overwhelming or confusing.

- Misinterpret emotional cues in others, resulting in misunderstandings.

- Experience delays in our emotional response, leading to confusion.

- Find it difficult to verbally express our emotions accurately.

- Rely on our logical thinking skills to get through stress.

In avoidant attachment, how we experience and express our emotions may be misunderstood. We don't choose to be uncaring. Our emotions, and therefore our ability to empathize, are hindered in ways we may struggle to control.[38]

What's important is understanding that our ability to feel and express emotions lies in how we are wired, which can be improved.

Since applying the technique I'll share with you in this chapter, I've learned so much about myself. I've gained the skills needed to face my emotions and actually feel them without shutting down or running away. My relationships can now sustain a healthier emotional climate with frequent sharing, understanding, and emotional connection. I now know when others are hurting and feel better equipped to show up for them in the same way I do for myself.

Our nervous systems are complex but forever adjusting to our thoughts, emotions, and behaviors.[39] By learning new ways to cope with stress, we can slowly allow ourselves to feel, identify, and express our emotions in healthier ways.

The second vital step toward breaking The Wall Of Detachment is nurturing emotional health. This will include a 6-step technique I like to call BEAR IT. It is an accumulation of all the exercises I used to transform my emotional health within myself and around others.

Emotional health is essential in secure relationships but involves multiple elements, including listening skills, emotional regulation, and more. If you're ready to feel the difference the BEAR IT Technique can make, read on.

STEP 2: NURTURE EMOTIONAL HEALTH

In avoidant attachment, we may have earned a reputation for being emotionally resilient and independent. But the way we appear to cope with emotional struggles doesn't necessarily represent our emotional health accurately. It may seem like being less sensitive to emotions and calmer in stressful situations is a strength. However, when we can't fully identify or express how we feel, we may struggle to apply appropriate levels of emotional regulation.[40]

For example, I could never get myself to reach out for support, even in situations where I knew social support would have been healthier than coping in isolation. I rarely took enough time to recover from stress and instead distracted myself with work or other less healthy coping mechanisms. My emotions felt restrained and distant. I came across as aloof when I wanted to show care and experienced a lack of empathy that damaged my relationships.

Without proper emotional regulation, our relationships can suffer. We may feel defensive in arguments and behave in dysregulated ways, shutting others out in an attempt to protect ourselves. This is why I've labeled our emotions defensive in The Wall Of Detachment.

Alexithymia and a lack of empathy may develop as a form of protection. We may fear fully experiencing and expressing our emotions and struggle to manage the closeness required for expressing genuine empathy. That's why we must nurture emotional health and develop the skills needed for powerful interpersonal relationships. We need to understand our emotions to better understand ourselves and then others.

Emotional health includes:

- Feeling emotions in a manageable way.

- Identifying and understanding our emotions.

- Regulating emotions with healthy coping skills.

- Expressing ourselves to others appropriately.

- Understanding and empathizing with others' emotions.

- Building emotional connections where we share openly.

Although this may seem like a lot, nurturing emotional health is a gradual process that the BEAR IT Technique can improve holistically. This technique can reduce levels of alexithymia, increase your empathy, and teach you healthier emotional regulation.[41] Instead of running away, I'll encourage you to embrace discomfort in the face of emotions, and BEAR IT.

The BEAR IT Technique: How To Transition From Emotional Suppression To Expression

In avoidant attachment, we experience urges to escape situations where we feel emotionally vulnerable. Our emotions may confuse us, creating the urge to regulate alone. Or, we may struggle to empathize with others, finding their emotions overwhelming. Whatever situation triggers the urge to escape or put our walls up, the underlying cause is the same: discomfort.

In the face of discomfort, we may reinforce our Wall Of Detachment with deactivating strategies. We exhibit These harmful behaviors when we disconnect from uncomfortable situations or relationships.[42] We will discuss these strategies further in Chapter 5. However, allowing our discomfort to justify these behaviors indicates poor emotional health.

There are healthier ways to cope.

To counteract our avoidant instincts and become more secure, we must learn to bear discomfort in a way that expands our comfort zone and teaches our nervous systems what emotional health feels like. This is where the BEAR IT Technique covers all the bases for nurturing emotional health in avoidant attachment. To BEAR IT and overcome defensive emotions, we can:

- **B**ecome self-aware with mindfulness.
- **A**ctively regulate our emotions.
- **E**mpathize with others and ourselves.
- **R**ecognize the whole truth with listening.

- **I**nvite discomfort to see growth.
- **T**alk openly and honestly.

Become Self-Aware With Mindfulness

To nurture emotional health, we must start by gaining a sensitivity to our emotions to experience them more fully. Much like we did with our thoughts, we can use mindfulness to gain a deeper sense of self-awareness. Mindfulness can help us feel more in touch with our thoughts and emotions. It helps us form the foundation necessary for improved emotional health. To practice mindfulness in a way that improves our emotional awareness, we can:

- **Breathe:** Take a moment to breathe deeply as you focus your awareness on your body.

- **Acknowledge sensations:** Notice any sensation you feel, such as warmth, tingling, increased heart rate, tension, or anything else that may indicate an emotion.

- **Question the experience:** Ask yourself questions like "Why do I feel this way?", "What happened just before?" and "What is my body trying to tell me?"

- **Label the emotion:** Think back to other times you've felt this way, consider the physiological sensations you've noticed, and see if you can label the emotion. If you're unsure, take a look at the emotions chart in your Workbook and pick a label closest to describing how you feel.

With time, this exercise can lead to a greater awareness of your emotions. They may start to feel more noticeable and physical. This is a good sign. It means your body no longer views emotions as a threat.[43]

Emotional awareness is not about becoming reactive but rather unlocking the fullness of our emotional lives to gain valuable insights into who we are and what we need. Our emotions are helpful indicators of what makes us feel good and what makes us tick.

Emotions are also essential when identifying boundaries. We will explore boundaries in depth in Part 3. For now, know that emotions are valuable. They are not something to escape but to process and learn from. To prevent harm, we can learn how to regulate them more actively.

Actively Regulate Emotions

As we start experiencing richer, more authentic emotions, we must regulate them without putting up our Wall Of Detachment, also known as deactivating. We need to form more active coping strategies to regulate our emotions. Depending on the emotion, some active regulation exercises include:

- **Ground yourself:** When you feel overwhelmed, focus on your senses. For example, you can focus on the texture of something in your hand, notice every green item in your environment, or count the number of sounds you hear. Try the exercise in your Workbook before you continue for a more in-depth grounding exercise you can use.

- **Process the emotion:** Once you've acknowledged and labeled the emotion, spend time with it. Allow your nervous system to work through it without suppressing it. You might do this by listening to music, journaling, or walking in nature. This is a vital step as it allows your nervous system to complete it's stress cycle, which it can become stuck in if we don't allow ourselves to feel the emotion and let it pass.[44]

- **Use your thoughts:** Apply what you learned in the previous chapter. Thoughts strongly influence emotions. You can use cognitive restructuring to get a handle on painful emotions by practicing a compassionate internal dialogue.

These simple regulation exercises will help you cope with discomfort without putting up your wall. They'll help you stay present with your emotions and gently improve your ability to cope even in the face of avoidant impulses.

Empathize With Others And Ourselves

As we learn to feel and process our emotions fully, it's important to show ourselves empathy. Emotions don't work with logic, and being hard on ourselves will not nurture the emotional health needed for secure relationships.

We also won't be perfect right away. We're destined to make mistakes and fall back into old patterns occasionally. That's why it's important we show others empathy too. We can practice empathy by:

- **Being patient:** We don't have to make drastic progress overnight, and we can't expect others to immediately notice a difference. Be patient with your expectations and prepare for gradual change.

- **Showing up:** Even in the face of change and struggle, showing up for ourselves and others is a way of expressing care. This can be both physically and emotionally. Your presence is powerful.

- **Practicing forgiveness:** Mistakes are inevitable. Being ready to forgive ourselves and others after mistakes shows empathy. Forgiveness doesn't mean forgetting the wrongs inflicted but rather letting go of grudges.

Empathy can be very practical. It's not always about fully understanding others' emotions. Sometimes, it's enough to recognize our humanity and choose to give grace. However, truly understanding another's perspective can go a long way.

Recognize The Whole Truth With Listening

When we're experiencing defensive emotions, listening can feel incredibly difficult. However, with the previous steps applied, it's important that we recognize the whole truth and not just our own. We need to hear the other person's perspective. Active listening is essential for helping others feel heard while we discover more pieces of the puzzle. To listen more actively, we can:

- Remove distractions like cell phones or TV.
- Focus on what someone is trying to say rather than simply hearing their words.
- Listen with the intention of gaining a new perspective without responding right away.
- Engage emotionally by showing care on your face and in your body language.
- Encourage more dialogue by asking open-ended questions like "I'd like to hear more so that I can truly understand." or "Is there anything else you'd like to share?"

Active listening is another great opportunity to show empathy. When we feel the urge to put our wall up, these steps can help us bear the discomfort and maintain connection. Maintaining a connection is essential because the experience is not one-sided.

When avoidant attachment is triggered, there is always someone else involved. This is when discomfort is a great ally.

Invite Discomfort To See Growth

There are nuances to discomfort. Not all discomfort indicates danger. Sometimes, discomfort signals the opportunity for growth. To truly nurture emotional health, we should expand our comfort zones. Growth is rarely easy, and discomfort is quick to trigger our defenses. However, we must learn to tolerate discomfort without engaging our avoidant impulses.

Invite discomfort into your life and use it as an indicator that you are challenging yourself. Of course, as we mentioned in Chapter 2, we don't want to break down The Wall Of Detachment too quickly, or else we risk feeling exposed and withdrawing further. Experiment with discomfort and learn to gauge your tolerance before being overwhelmed.

A quick note: This only applies in healthy situations where your discomfort results from avoidant attachment, not genuine harm.

Talk Openly And Honestly

Regardless of how confusing or disproportionate they may seem, your emotions are valid. That makes them an essential part of any healthy relationship. The final portion of the BEAR IT Technique is expressing your emotions. That means talking openly and honestly about how you feel. Let these communication tips help you out:

- Pause and take your time to respond, especially when emotionally charged.

- Start by sharing basic feelings and work your way up to deeper emotions.

- Be as clear and intentional with what you say as possible.

- Acknowledge discomfort and be honest about your emotions.

- Use non-verbal body language to engage and show vulnerability.

- Use "I" statements to take full responsibility for your emotions. Examples include "I feel unheard when you talk over me " and "I need 10 minutes alone to help me cope."

In Part 3, we will discuss communication and how to best apply these tips during conflict. But for now, the BEAR IT Technique will help you nurture emotional health as we continue. Take a moment to visit your Workbook and complete the exercise I've prepared for you. It will bring this technique together and paint a workable example of when and how to use it.

CONCLUSION

Despite the negative reputation we may attract for having an avoidant attachment style, our difficulties in feeling, expressing, and empathizing with emotions are not intentional. It's in the way we're wired.

But that doesn't mean we can't change.

We must nurture emotional health to heal defensive emotions and express them rather than suppress them. While there are many elements to emotional health, the BEAR IT Technique can train us to:

- Become self-aware
- Actively regulate emotions
- Empathize with others and ourselves
- Recognize the whole truth by listening
- Invite discomfort to see growth
- Talk openly and honestly

This technique is enough to experience improved levels of alexithymia and empathy. It's enough to help us embrace discomfort in relationships when we know it's best for us. Nurturing emotional health can help us feel more open and willing to share our true feelings while overcoming fears.

However, thoughts and emotions are tightly linked with behaviors.[45] They may be responsible for our urges to deactivate and keep our distance. The same is true in reverse. Behavioral impulses and their results can quickly tear down our improving mindset and trigger old emotional patterns. That's why the next layer we must address is our deactivating behaviors.

In the next chapter, you will learn Step 3, which includes how to recognize an avoidant behavioral pattern or deactivating strategy and consciously manage your behavior to improve your relationships. If you're ready to feel a lasting change, turn the page.

DEACTIVATING BEHAVIORS: RECOGNIZING THE PATTERNS

Catching Yourself In The Act

"Relationships often reflect back to us the quality of our own thinking and behavior."

– Beau Norton

THE IMPORTANCE OF SELF-AWARENESS: WHY IT'S THE ULTIMATE HEALING TOOL

A lack of self-awareness is only visible in hindsight. When I would rush off to work to avoid conflict, talk myself out of furthering a relationship, or hold back emotionally during key relationship milestones, it felt right. Only once I developed more self-awareness did I realize that my behavior wasn't okay. It was destroying my relationships.

I couldn't see it then. When I felt uncomfortable in relationships, I went into protection mode. My Wall Of Detachment was fortified, and there was nothing anyone could say to wobble it. My wall was there for me, and it made sense at the time. Breaking it down felt like doing myself an injustice.

However, after my failed engagement with someone I really loved, I had to rethink everything I "knew" to be true about relationships. It started with my mindset, moved on to managing my emotional health, and then led me to something incredibly difficult. I had to question the avoidant behaviors that I felt were genuine.

Why would I change if I genuinely felt like my behavior was warranted?

The truth is, I had to make a choice. I could either continue fighting for my independence at the expense of good relationships or surrender to new outcomes. I wanted to experience the warmth and joy a progressing relationship could bring. Deep down, I was sick of being so alone. But addressing my behaviors wasn't as simple as choosing new ones and following through. When a situation would trigger my avoidant attachment, it was as if the old me took over. I felt like I was doing what was best and had little control over doing things differently, even when "what was best" was exiting a healthy relationship.

This is where self-awareness changed my life.

Self-awareness is less about noticing what you're doing and more about understanding why. It's about having the insight into yourself that allows for a deeper sense of control. When we can see our behavioral patterns for what they are – behaviors we are wired to repeat – we gain the power to unlearn them and instill new patterns.

Much like changing negative thought patterns, we can reeducate ourselves to behave in healthier ways. This isn't possible when we can't see past our own walls. But self-awareness is a looking glass that allows us to see beyond our limitations. And developing a deeper sense of self-awareness, regardless of where you stand now, is entirely possible.[46]

In this chapter, we will explore common avoidant behaviors, also known as deactivating strategies, before working through essential exercises designed to build self-awareness. Together, each exercise will guide you through the 3rd step towards breaking The Wall Of Detachment: Resolving the deactivating behaviors that keep us alone.

STEP 3: RECOGNIZE PATTERNS AND REACTIVATE

Negative behavioral patterns in avoidant attachment are known as deactivating strategies because when we engage in them, we deactivate from the situation, others, and even ourselves. They include any behaviors that disconnect us, reduce positive thoughts or emotions, remove us from a healthy situation, or cause resistance toward positive change.[47] Deactivating strategies have also been shown to decrease emotional self-awareness and self-compassion.[48]

These negative behavioral patterns can include:

- **Deliberate Emotional Distance:** Avoiding deep or emotional conversations to keep relationships superficial.

- **Downplaying Emotions:** Minimizing or dismissing our own and others' feelings to avoid vulnerability.

- **Conflict Avoidance And Stonewalling:** Purposefully avoiding conflict by physically leaving tense situations or shutting down emotionally, also known as stonewalling.[49]

- **Escapist Coping Mechanisms:** Coping with relationship stress by escaping into video games, TV, substance use, or other unhealthy coping mechanisms.

- **Using Boundaries As Walls:** Setting rigid and unrealistic boundaries that prevent emotional closeness in relationships.

- **Overindulging In Personal Space:** Justifying and overindulging the need for space to avoid closeness.

- **External Preoccupations:** Keeping ourselves preoccupied with activities outside the relationship, like work and hobbies, to avoid spending time with loved ones.

- **Reducing Disconnecting Behavior:** Brushing off our disconnecting behaviors as minor problems or unproblematic.

- **Negative Internal Dialogue:** Talking ourselves out of positive relationship experiences using negative internal dialogue like "It's not worth my effort."

- **Exaggerating Others' Flaws:** Fixating on others' flaws and exaggerating them in our minds to justify emotional distance or detachment.

- **Blaming External Circumstances:** Attributing relationship problems to external stressors like work stress or bad timing to avoid accountability.

- **Resentful Compliance:** Reluctantly agreeing to relationship milestones and commitments, leading to passive-aggressive behavior later on.

- **Deflecting Affection:** Dismissing or avoiding compliments, affection, or expressions of love from a partner to avoid reinforcing positive emotions in the relationship.

- **Relationship Sabotage:** Purposefully engaging in hurtful behaviors like flirting or unreasonable conflict in an attempt to end a relationship.

- **Ghosting:** Cutting off contact or disappearing from someone's life with little or no explanation when the relationship becomes too serious.

I once used many, if not all, of these behaviors to keep myself secure in relationships. And in the moment, each of them felt valid and right. I didn't consider that they may not be best for me or my relationships until things went wrong. However, even when they feel appropriate, there are very few circumstances where these behaviors are okay. For example, stonewalling can be considered emotional abuse in extreme cases.[50] It's vital we recognize behavioral patterns and break free from their hold.

We must learn to recognize when we are deactivating to bypass our limitations and choose healthier, active behaviors. If we want to become more secure in relationships, we can no longer rely on behaviors that keep us in our comfort zones. We must act in new ways that may initially feel uncomfortable, using our growing self-awareness to persevere.

I didn't want to change at first, but the heartbreak I endured was the push I needed. All I can ask is that you read on with an open mind and consider the exercises I'll share before you're forced into change through painful circumstances, too. And if you are here battling heartbreak, you're here; keep going.

With self-awareness, we can gain control over our behaviors and feel more motivated to change, even when growth feels challenging. However, self-awareness isn't always easy to learn because it's an invisible skill. It's not something we can easily learn by example because it takes experience to understand it. The exercises I'll encourage you to do next will put you in the perfect position to experience and build self-awareness while resolving deactivating behaviors.

These 4 exercises will help you identify the situations, moments, and emotions that trigger deactivating strategies so you can take actionable steps toward growth. They will also help you resolve these behaviors and reactive yourself for better relationship outcomes.

Exercise 1: Notice The Avoidant Impulse

In avoidant attachment, what triggers our deactivating behavior may not be obvious. Our initial response to a trigger may feel natural and warranted, making it tough to see our behavior as harmful. But how do we differentiate between triggers and a fair response to threats?

When we're triggered, the impulse to act will be intense and feel overly urgent in relation to the "threat." In avoidant attachment, anything from an intimate look to a big proposal can be mistaken for a threat. To differentiate a healthy response from a deactivating behavior, we can notice our avoidant impulses and consider whether they match the intensity or validity of the threat.

For example, if someone treats you poorly and criticizes you, following through on a strong urge to leave would be warranted and not indicate deactivating behavior. But if your partner expresses their love for you and you then experience and follow through on the same urge, it would indicate deactivating behavior. However, many other normal relationship interactions may trigger deactivating behavior, which we will discuss in Exercise 3.

Some fears may be normal during big relationship milestones, like moving in together, but noticing our impulses can give us the choice to follow through with them or not. It can give us the self-awareness to consider what we really want and help us find enough control to change our behaviors for the better.

Avoidant impulses can be easiest to recognize as they are often the first sign we are about to deactivate. They're the initial knee-jerk response to perceived relationship threats. Noticing them gives us a world of insight into our triggers and behavioral patterns.

Common avoidant impulses include the impulse to:

- **Withdraw:** A strong impulse to physically or emotionally retreat from a situation that feels too intimate or demanding.

- **Deflect:** Wanting to change the subject when the conversation requests personal information or emotional topics.

- **Downplay:** Needing to minimize the significance of the relationship, your feelings, or your partner's feelings to maintain emotional distance.

- **Justify:** Feeling an internal drive to rationalize needing space or pulling away to avoid feeling guilty or taking responsibility.

- **Blame:** A temptation to shift the responsibility for discomfort onto your partner or external circumstances.

- **Criticise:** Experiencing a mental shift that wants to focus on your partner's flaws or mistakes, using them as an excuse to disengage.

- **Escape:** A sudden urge to engage in activities that take your mind off the relationship or any feelings related to it.

- **Dismiss:** An inclination to invalidate a partner's feelings, pushing them away emotionally.

Consider the deactivating behaviors we listed previously. Can you see how they are always preceded by an impulse? It might feel confronting, but when we experience an impulse, following through is our choice. However, noticing the impulse can be enough to gain control and choose differently.

Think back to a recent event in which you deactivated in an otherwise healthy situation. See if you can identify which impulse you experienced before the behavior. Make a note in your Workbook, and move on to exercise 2.

Exercise 2: Label The Emotion

When triggered, our emotions often exacerbate our impulses. That's why labeling them is important in resolving deactivating behaviors. When we label our emotions, we can regulate them appropriately and behave more constructively.

As we discussed in Chapter 4, alexithymia may inhibit our ability to feel or identify emotions. This is another opportunity for you to practice the techniques learned in Chapter 4 to continue building emotional self-awareness.

Refer back to the first step of the BEAR IT Technique, where you applied mindfulness to help you acknowledge sensations, question your experience, and label your emotions using an emotions chart.

Emotions are also a powerful messenger. Because they produce a physiological response, they may be a more accessible resource for us as we develop self-awareness. When we feel sensations, such as an increased heart rate, muscle tension, or a shift in body language, we can pay attention and learn how our bodies feel when triggered.

Your Workbook includes a list of common physiological signs to help expand your emotional awareness. Consider which emotions indicate a trigger response for you and write them in your Workbook before the next exercise.

Exercise 3: Identify The Trigger

Once we've gained enough insight into our impulses and emotions, we can identify the situations that trigger our deactivating behaviors. We can consider the interaction, circumstance, or experience moments before we feel the avoidant impulse.

This is the most important part of this step.

Knowing our triggers can help us face them more actively before they sweep us into a whirlwind of emotions, impulses, and harmful behaviors. Some common triggers for deactivating behaviors include situations that create:[51]

- Intimacy or closeness, both emotionally or physically.
- Vulnerability, such as sharing feelings.
- Perceived loss of independence.
- Feeling emotionally or physically smothered.
- Conflict or confrontation, even when it's healthy.
- High emotional demand in relationships.
- Intense emotional expression or experience.

If it isn't already clear what triggered us, we can analyze our internal dialogue for clues. When we are triggered, our thoughts may fixate on the problem or start deactivating internal dialogue related to the problem. Your workbook includes an exercise to help you identify triggers using your internal dialogue. Complete that now before continuing to the next exercise.

Exercise 4: Reactivate

Once we've identified our triggers and have gained enough awareness and control over them, we can reactivate by choosing a more active, engaging response. For example, instead of:

- Deliberate Emotional Distance (Arrow to right) Gradual Emotional Engagement

- Downplaying Emotions (Arrow to right) Validating Emotions

- Conflict Avoidance And Stonewalling (Arrow to right) Constructive Conflict Resolution

- Escapist Coping Mechanisms (Arrow to right) Healthy Stress Management

- Using Boundaries As Walls (Arrow to right) Setting Clear, Reasonable Boundaries

- Overindulging In Personal Space (Arrow to right) Balancing Alone Time Fairly

- External Preoccupations (Arrow to right) Prioritizing Our Relationships Appropriately

- Reducing Deactivating Behavior (Arrow to right) Acknowledging Deactivating Behavior

- Negative Internal Dialogue (Arrow to right) Practicing Positive Self-talk

- Exaggerating Others Flaws (Arrow to right) Noticing Strengths And Showing Appreciation

- Blaming External Circumstances (Arrow to right) Taking Responsibility For Emotions

- Resentful Compliance (Arrow to right) Making Authentic Decisions

- Deflecting Affection (Arrow to right) Accepting Love And Affection

- Relationship Sabotage (Arrow to right) Ending Relationships Fairly

- Ghosting (Arrow to right) Honest And Compassionate Communication.

What constitutes reactivating behavior is self-compassion and compassion for others. Our behaviors should reflect the people we want to be, not our wounds. This doesn't mean we can't be ourselves or act authentically, only that we choose to act in accordance with the outcome we're hoping for. In Dialectical Behavioral Therapy (DBT), a sister therapy of CBT based on behavior rather than thoughts, reactivating is also known as opposite action.[52] I've included an opposite action exercise in your Workbook to help solidify this vital practice.

Reactivating In Action

Here are some examples of how reactivating can save an uncomfortable situation from damaging our relationships:

- Validating Emotions: When our partners express their emotions during conflict, we can use phrases like "I hear you" or "So, you're feeling XYZ, is there anything I can do?" This puts us in an active position to connect with our partners and show we care.

- Prioritizing Our Relationships Appropriately: Knowing that healthy relationships require time and energy to maintain, we can prioritize our relationships by making a time commitment to the relationship each week. This may be dedicating a certain time of day, or one full day a week to fully engage with the relationship.

- Acknowledging Deactivating Behavior: When we catch ourselves deactivating, it's likely to have already impacted our partners in some way. To remedy their hurt and hold ourselves accountable, we can simply acknowledge our behavior. We might say "I know I tend to pull away, I'm sorry. I am trying not to." This can forge a deeper understanding of each others experience and reassure our partners that their hurt is valid.

- Accepting Love And Affection: When our partners express their feelings for us or initiate physical affection, we can consider how our partners are safe people to indulge in affection with. We don't necessarily need to do much after this, other than allow it and enjoy it!

- Honest And Compassionate Communication: If we're feeling smothered or unhappy in a relationship, it's important that we communicate honestly and compassionately with our partners. This will give us the opportunity to express how we feel and others the opportunity to understand and learn from what went wrong. We will dive further into compassionate communication in Chapter 6.

With our mindset and emotional health in place, we will begin to recognize how valuable good relationships are and want to resolve our deactivating behaviors. By this point in the book, I trust you're seeing how possible and necessary healing is. I hope you feel motivated to apply what you've learned and keep deconstructing your wall like I did. I know this journey is worth it. I want you to know that, too.

CONCLUSION

With the steps throughout these last three chapters in motion, you're creating the ideal environment for self-awareness to develop wholly and fully. Your mindset is slowly becoming more secure, your emotional health is growing, and you're resolving and reactivating your behaviors. You're creating room for good relationships in your life. And although it may be uncomfortable, it's also fantastic.

Addressing your deactivating behaviors is the final fundamental step in breaking The Wall Of Detachment. When you can catch your impulses, emotions, and triggers before they become deactivating behaviors, you've done enough work for others to start seeing behind your wall. With your reactivating behaviors put into practice, you will gradually feed your relationships with an authentic sense of engagement.

However, the journey doesn't end here.

The more our walls come down and our relationships develop, the more our fears will challenge us. We open ourselves up to more triggers but also more potential for growth. This is where facing our fears is the next essential step to breaking The Wall Of Detachment for the long term. In the next chapter, we will address the first of our two dominant fears in avoidant attachment – vulnerability – and explore practical ways to overcome it.

6

THE COURAGE TO BE VULNERABLE

My First Steps Towards Opening Up

"Never close your lips to those whom you have already opened your heart."

– Charles Dickens

THE FREEDOM OF VULNERABILITY

My mouth was dry as a bone. I knew I was running out of time. My partner had almost finished his dinner, and I had to speak up. I'd committed myself to intentionally acknowledging one good thing my partner had done in the day. Vulnerability has always been difficult for me, and this was my way of practicing emotional openness. But it was my first time trying the exercise, and I felt stumped.

I clamored with my thoughts. They were whirling around in a slew of "I don't want to do this" and "Is this even worth it?" My stomach was a pit. But I had to follow through. I was already deep enough in my healing journey to realize how much this simple exercise would nourish my relationship.

Almost stammering, I said, "Hey, babe?"

"Yeah?"

Taking his hand, I tried to sink myself into the present. I looked him in the eyes and told him how much I appreciated his dedication to cooking dinner for us every night. It was an easy thing to recognize and it definitely helped that we were just finishing another dinner he'd cooked. I took my chance to make it seem natural and not premeditated. The results surprised me.

Like watching a child open the birthday present they'd been wishing for, his face gleamed, and his entire demeanor transformed. I might've gotten quieter after that, but it didn't matter. The rest of the night was filled with light-hearted jokes and good energy between us. We felt more connected in a way that didn't scare me as much as I thought it would.

I always assumed that becoming more vulnerable with my partners would cause an inescapable drive for more openness. I worried that expressing myself would be a slippery slope to uncomfortable levels of closeness and seriousness. But instead, it did something unexpected. It eased the tension I didn't realize was there. My partner felt seen and appreciated. He didn't need to pressure me for more. The appreciation I showed was enough – at least for the short term.

I quickly learned that keeping up with my vulnerability practice leads to great things. The patterns of neediness and pressure I often noticed in my partner drastically decreased, and I spent far less time feeling triggered to deactivate. Facing my fear of vulnerability in this way helped me gradually overcome something that limited me for most of my life.

It didn't take sharing my innermost thoughts and desires straight away, either.

The most basic display of appreciation unfolded into a healthier, more vulnerable communication pattern in my relationship. I was able to expand my comfort zone slowly and open up in a way that didn't shut me down. This was the start of a deeper, more comfortable connection with my partner. And it's what allowed my relationship to progress and grow into what it is today – one of the biggest sources of light in my life.

With the first 3 layers of The Wall Of Detachment dissolving, you're ready to start facing your fears. This is where you turn towards your avoidant attachment and separate yourself from it. It's where you experience the pull of detachment and actively expand your comfort zone for a fuller, freer life.

For Step 4, I'm going to share my most impactful techniques for overcoming our doubt about vulnerability, including gradual exposure, communication ice-breakers, and my personal daily vulnerability practice. Summon up the courage to use what you've learned up until this point in combination with these techniques. It will change your relationship dynamics forever, in the best possible way.

STEP 4: OVERCOME DOUBT TO OPEN UP

In avoidant attachment, our aversion to vulnerability may not feel like fear in our bodies, but truthfully it is. That's why we must approach opening up in the same way we would approach overcoming other fears like a fear of heights or social anxiety. We must gradually expose ourselves to discomfort to expand our comfort zones and find freedom.

Being courageous is not about squashing fear before taking action, it's about taking action despite it.

When I started opening up, I had to force myself. It wasn't comfortable, and it didn't always go well. But it didn't take long before I recognized the value in what I was doing. I tried my best to overlook my present discomfort and trust the process of my journey. At first, I had to muster up the courage to be vulnerable each time I followed through with my vulnerability practice.

But as my relationship grew, rather than becoming increasingly uncomfortable, I became increasingly happy and secure.

Opening up fed a deep need that I didn't know I had: the need to be seen, heard, and understood for who I am. With the first three layers of my Wall Of Detachment dissolving, vulnerability was my ticket to healing the core wounds from which my wall formed.

Before we get into the techniques I'm about to share, it's important to understand why we may doubt the value of vulnerability. As we discussed in Chapter 2, avoidant attachment forms from the false or limiting beliefs we obtain from our primary caregivers. If you refer back to these beliefs, there is a recurring theme: They each instill a fear of vulnerability in us in various ways. For example, how can we be vulnerable when we:

- Don't trust others with our feelings?
- Believe opening up will lead to rejection?
- See closeness as a threat?
- Think dependency makes us weak?
- Believe trust will lead to disappointment?
- Don't believe our needs are important?
- Prioritize performance over true love?

The techniques in this chapter will allow you to face these limiting beliefs and push through them. They will put you in situations where you will feel uncomfortable. But this is where their effectiveness begins. If you embrace the discomfort and face your limiting beliefs, fears, and doubts, your openness will pay off. Practicing vulnerability is the only way to overcome the fear of it. It's the only way to learn more about it and see what it's worth.

However, we don't want to break our walls down too quickly. The success of Step 4 lies in a steady approach. Consistency beats scale in these techniques. This isn't about forcing openness in a way that drives you further away from vulnerability. It's about actively deciding to expand your comfort zone slowly and productively. These are the 3 techniques you can apply today:

Gradual Exposure

Gradual exposure therapy is a useful yet courageous approach to overcoming irrational fears.[53] Unlike avoidance, where we prefer to avoid situations that make us uncomfortable, gradual exposure encourages us to purposefully place ourselves in situations where we can experience discomfort in a safe and manageable way.[54] Then, as we become comfortable with these situations, we gradually increase the intensity of the exercise until we make marked progress.

For example, you might start by sharing something on the LearnWell Community to gradually open up with others.

In avoidant attachment, the situations that make us uncomfortable will vary in intensity. This will influence where you start on your exposure journey. For example, I might find conversations about emotions more triggering than conversations about my ideas and opinions. Therefore, I will start by gradually exposing myself to conversations about my ideas and opinions before tackling conversations about my emotions. You might experience things differently.

What's important is that you accurately gauge which healthy acts of vulnerability trigger your avoidant attachment and the intensity of their impact. Any expression of your needs may trigger avoidant behaviors because of our inherent need to be independent. But it's important to let others in if we want our connections to thrive. Consider this list of my personal triggering acts of vulnerability listed from the least impactful to most impactful:

- **Share minor, physical discomforts.** For example, "I've got a headache" or "My chair is uncomfortable."

- **Express preferences in low-stakes situations.** For example, "I'd rather stay home than go out to eat tonight." or "I'd prefer a comedy movie."

- **Ask for help with simple tasks.** For example, "Can you help carry these groceries in?" or "I'm not sure how to fold this sheet properly, can you try?"

- **Share an opinion or insight.** For example, "I'm not a fan of detective stories." or "Tom Cruise must not be afraid of heights like I am."

- **Acknowledge mild emotional states.** For example, "I feel a little off today." or "Work is stressing me out a bit."

- **Admit to a mistake or oversight.** For example, "I spilled coffee on my shirt." or "I forgot to pick up laundry detergent."

- **Share a goal or aspiration.** For example, "I'd like to learn at least 3 languages in my lifetime." or "I'm aiming for a promotion at work."

- **Reveal a personal fear or insecurity.** For example, "I'm afraid of letting people in." or "Sometimes I don't feel like I'm good enough."

- **Expressing affection or love.** For example, "I really care about you." or "I love spending time with you."

- **Discuss deep emotional struggles.** For example, "A negative experience from the past has been bothering me lately." or "I feel incredibly overwhelmed today."

Some of my least impactful expressions of vulnerability may not seem relevant to most people, but sharing our physical discomfort or asking for help can be extremely difficult in avoidant attachment. We may believe those expressions aren't important, but in reality, they give others opportunities to get to know us. With my list in mind, head to your Workbook and fill out your personal list. It doesn't matter how silly the act of vulnerability may seem, if it triggers discomfort, it's relevant. You will need this to refer back to when practicing gradual exposure.

Now that you have your ordered list of vulnerable acts, act on them! Start at the top of your list and actively implement them into your life. Expect discomfort but don't let it stop you from trying. Notice it, acknowledge it, and embrace it. Use what you learned in Chapter 4 to help you persevere through uncomfortable emotions and take note of the positive outcomes that follow.

Once your discomfort regarding a vulnerable act has consistently lowered by around 50%, move down to the next, more challenging act on your list. Repeat the process until you're consistently tackling each situation on your list without as much avoidance.

Don't rush it. Take your time and see it as a lifelong transition to becoming more vulnerable.

Starting A Daily Vulnerability Practice

Once you've become adept at gradually exposing yourself to situations that require vulnerability, you can take things up a notch and start a vulnerability practice. As in my story, a daily vulnerability practice radically improved my relationships. To start, decide on one simple yet challenging way to open up with your partner every day. Consider your partner's needs, or what you could share that would add to your connection. For example, you could:

- Pay attention to the good your partner does and challenge yourself to express gratitude for one thing every day.

- Notice what your partner gets frustrated about and make a point of verbally acknowledging their feelings before helping them solve the problem.

- Choose to verbally express your emotions when they come up even when they're negative, then allow your partner to comfort you.

- Make an effort to directly express affection and love for your partner in ways they will receive well. For example, if words of affirmation are their love language, express yourself in words! We will discuss love languages in the next technique.

- Ask your partner to assist you with something you may or may not genuinely need help with. For example, if you're cooking dinner, invite your partner to join you in the kitchen even if you don't need them to. Use the activity to initiate quality time together.

A daily vulnerability practice is an intentional step towards opening up. It is a daily commitment you make to becoming more vulnerable. Choose one thing you can do daily for the next week to kick off your vulnerability practice. Use the space in your Workbook to reflect on your relationships and write down at least 3 personal ways you can open up. Use this list to hold yourself accountable and remind yourself of your commitments.

Remember, this isn't just a commitment to building up your relationships but also a commitment to yourself. You've made it this far because a part of you is hungry for growth. A daily vulnerability practice is a great way to continue showing up on this journey.

Icebreakers For Vulnerable Communication

As people who may experience detached thinking patterns, emotional shutdown, and deactivating impulses, it helps to feel prepared. We can memorize these icebreakers for initiating vulnerable communication to help us start off on the right track. There are three avenues of vulnerability we should prepare to initiate in healthy relationships.

Positive Reinforcement For The Relationship

Even though we love our partners, it isn't always easy to initiate positive conversations without inspiration. Depending on your and your partner's love languages, you can tailor your approach to fully satisfy each other's needs. Love languages are our individual preferences for giving and receiving love. There is a definition for each of the 5 love languages in your Workbook. Review them before we continue.

To initiate positive reinforcement in your relationships, you might like to try the following icebreakers depending on your partner's love language:

- **Positive touch.** For example, if your partner's love language is physical affection, they might respond best to gentle physical touches like hand-holding or hugs. Becoming more vulnerable doesn't always require words.

- **Words of affirmation.** For example, you can be vulnerable with your partner by making an effort to speak words of affirmation around them, such as "I love your outfit today" or "You always tell the best jokes."

- **Quality time.** For example, planning an activity with your partner where they will have your undivided attention may be a powerful way to initiate deeper conversations.

- **Gifts.** For example, giving your partner a thoughtful gift can communicate your feelings for them in a way that words may not be able to describe.

- **Acts of service.** We may be accustomed to showing our love through acts of service, but there are ways to make this love language a vulnerability practice. For example, rather than helping our partners with a task in private, we can ask them what they need help with. We can also initiate acts of service that require us to work with our partners.

Difficult Discussions And Conflict

When we are well-prepared to initiate and handle healthy conflict, we no longer need to avoid it. Positively initiating conflict can drastically improve our interaction and give our partners the reassurance they need in advance. Next time you need to bring something difficult up with your partner, try these icebreakers:

- **"I" Statements:** These are a great way to initiate conflict without blaming or avoiding accountability. For example, "I feel frustrated by the state of the kitchen. Can we talk about solutions?" or "I have a lot of things on my mind. Are you open to helping me work through them?"

- **Acknowledge Positive Intentions:** Before getting into difficult topics or confrontations, we can start by acknowledging our partners' positive intentions. For example, "I know you mean well when you check up on me at work, but can we discuss limiting checkups to text only?" or "You're such a caring person, but sometimes it's okay to let me process my emotions alone."

- **Seek, Don't State:** Statements can feel confrontational as they may imply many things that can offend or put our partners on edge. However, if we initiate conflict by seeking our partners' support, we can enter conflict in problem-solving mode. For example, "I'd really like your perspective on something I've been struggling with in the relationship." or "I feel like there's been some tension between us this week, I'd like to understand what's been going on for both of us."

Reaching Out For Help And Support

As devotedly independent people, asking for help and support may be the most challenging vulnerability practice. However, you can use these icebreakers to help you reach out when support will make your life and relationship better:

- **Affirm Your Partner's Importance:** When we need to ask for help or support, we can start by affirming our partners' importance to encourage a positive reply. For example, "I trust you more than most people, and your insight into this problem would mean a lot to me." or "You're always there for me when I need support. I'm struggling with something big right now and would love your input. Do you have time to talk?"

- **Express Your Difficulty Asking For Help:** Simply sharing how difficult we find asking for help is incredibly vulnerable and will likely encourage empathy. For example, "I don't normally ask for help, but right now I feel like I could use it." or "This is hard for me as I'd prefer to handle it alone, but I'm realizing I need support. Can we talk?"

- **Appreciate Their Support:** When asking for help feels like a burden on others, focus on showing your appreciation for their support. For example, "You've always been so good at supporting me, I could really use your support right now." or "Your help and support in the past has been the most impactful for me, can you help me work through something now?"

These icebreakers open the door for us to be vulnerable with others. They can help us cut past the overthinking that may happen when we enter a vulnerable situation. Instead of listening to our deactivating impulses and negative internal dialogue, we can use these icebreakers to communicate vulnerably in seconds.

Opening up and being vulnerable is challenging for most people. It can leave us exposed to criticism, rejection, and disappointment. But with avoidant attachment, vulnerability isn't just challenging; it feels threatening. That's why we must practice vulnerability like we're overcoming a major fear.

With consistency and a true desire to see progress, these 3 techniques can help us open up and reap the benefits of vulnerability in our relationships. They can help us feel seen, heard, and understood by our partners so that we aren't as guarded.

I'd also like to acknowledge that by this point in your journey, changes in your beliefs and behaviors may influence changes in your partner. In Part 3, we will discuss why it's important to get our partners involved in our healing journey, including how we can navigate this inclusion effectively.

CONCLUSION

Although I saw progress and managed to maintain a new relationship after starting my healing journey, it was vulnerability that deepened the connection and reinforced it. However, the reinforcements vulnerability can offer don't last forever. We must consistently and actively practice vulnerability to find lasting fulfillment in relationships.

The 3 techniques I shared with you don't require huge time commitments or sacrifice. They are the kinds of techniques that you can apply daily and consistently in small yet impactful ways. They include:

- **Gradual exposure:** Where you can gently face the vulnerable situations triggering your avoidant thoughts, emotions, and behaviors, starting from the least challenging to the most. This is where you begin overcoming any fears or resistance.

- **A daily vulnerability practice:** Where you make a daily commitment to vulnerably express yourself in a way that's bound to uplift the relationship.

- **Icebreakers for vulnerable communication:** Where you learn and memorize prompts to initiate healthy, vulnerable conversations in your relationship, including conflict, seeking support, and positive reinforcement.

While simple and small, these techniques can significantly improve our relationships. Especially when a lack of vulnerability has suffocated our emotional connections. Practiced regularly and consistently, they can foster a deeper understanding between partners, encourage improved conflict resolution, and nurture positive feelings. They help us become more open, aware, and willing to share our experiences as we begin to recognize the value of vulnerability.

But vulnerability naturally makes way for another ingrained fear in avoidant attachment: Intimacy. With our Wall Of Detachment crumbling by the day, our comfort zones are expanding and making room for more. This is where I urge you to continue pushing forward. With the final layer left to stand, relationships can only progress so far. They may be deeper, but they will be lacking something vital to fulfilling and lasting connections. If you're ready to finish what you started and learn to love closeness like I did, turn the page.

INTIMACY BOOTCAMP

How I Learned To Stop Fearing
And Love Closeness

*"True love is not a hide and seek game:
in true love, both lovers seek each other."*

– Michael Bassey Johnson

ESTABLISHING AN ENVIRONMENT WHERE INTIMACY CAN FEEL COMFORTABLE

Sex was a meaningless act. I could indulge in it without an ounce of my heart. While I was okay with this empty exchange, my partners were left with much less. They often felt used, neglected, and unsure of my feelings about them.

In relationships, I would allow our connection to grow just enough for physical intimacy to become viable. This made for longer lasting yet emotionally dysfunctional relationships. I didn't want to be alone. I valued connection just as much as anyone, but only to the extent that the reward outweighed the risk. This imbalance of enough physical intimacy without much emotional intimacy felt like the sweet spot for my avoidant attachment. The trouble was, it earned me a reputation for stringing partners along.

This accusation wasn't entirely false. While my intentions were never to hurt or use anyone, I did. But I didn't understand what was happening at the time. Looking back, I realize that my resistance to emotional intimacy was an attempt to protect myself from the incredible risk that comes with loving someone fully. The risk of losing them, feeling the sting of rejection or abandonment. I truly believed that it was for the best. But I was wrong.

My emotional withdrawal, paired with a willingness for physical intimacy, did more damage than I expected. My approach had risks I'd overlooked. In the long term, a lack of emotional intimacy cost me gravely. It did to others what I was fearing for myself. I hurt people and have never been shown forgiveness by most of them.

I now know that avoiding intimacy out of fear of rejection, abandonment, or closeness is the risky choice. It leaves a relationship hollow and unfulfilling. It hurts others, and deep down, it hurts us, too. Since lowering my defenses and becoming more vulnerable, I've realized that intimacy, especially emotional intimacy, is vital for reaping the most rewards from relationships.

As people who tend to focus on risk reduction in relationships, we owe it to ourselves to continue healing. After years of stringing people along and maintaining relationships without longevity in mind, I needed to change. With the help of my therapist and years of trial and error, I've come to a place where my partner's tender gaze doesn't make me want to look away, words of affirmation no longer go unappreciated, and the gentle touches we exchange set my heart on fire.

My love is whole, and I'm allowing myself to experience it fully.

Now that you've reached a point along this journey where your Wall Of Detachment is no longer blocking people out, it's time to clear the path and remove the final hurdle standing in the way of a secure, fulfilling connection. Don't let intimacy stay skin-deep like I did. Let it touch your heart, warm it, and let it burn with a love you've never allowed before.

With the vulnerability we've opened up to in Chapter 6, intimacy isn't far behind. You've already begun building an environment where intimacy can feel natural and comfortable. For Step 5, we will expand our openness and cultivate closeness. This is where our fears of dependency, rejection, and many others may flare. So keep reading, and let's explore the solutions that helped me both cultivate and absolutely love closeness.

STEP 5: CULTIVATE CLOSENESS

Our aversion to intimacy will be unique. While I managed to engage in physical intimacy, provided that I stayed emotionally distant, you might experience things differently. Our experiences will vary depending on our fears, beliefs, and comfort zones. Whatever form of intimacy we equate to increased closeness will likely be what we avoid. We may even avoid intimacy altogether. The two types of intimacy include:

- **Physical intimacy:** while this includes sex, it also includes any form of connecting touch like hand-holding, cuddling, or even gently touching someone's arm.

- **Emotional intimacy:** emotionally connecting behaviors, words, and non-physical activity such as deep conversation, positive body language, and quality time.[55]

There is a notable overlap between physical intimacy and emotional intimacy. For example, loving touch between partners can forge a deeper emotional connection in the same way that words of affirmation may be delivered best with gentle physical contact. That's why it's important to nurture and practice both forms of intimacy. For Step 5, we need to cultivate closeness in a way that makes us want to draw nearer to our partners both physically and emotionally. Let these 5 solutions guide you:

Solution 1: Trust

Trust is an essential solution for cultivating closeness. When someone trusts us, and we trust them, intimacy can unfold without question. We don't have to wonder about the sincerity of the experience.

In the previous chapter, we learned a toolbox of vulnerability practices. Practiced consistently, these are bound to build trust. However, there are other integral ways that we can lay a foundation of trust that comfortably supports closeness. Trust is built over time and with repeated success. It's built with consistency and reliability.

If we stand by the following rules, we will position ourselves as trustworthy people, even if we've spent years emotionally neglecting relationships:

- **Always show up in hard times:** When someone we love is going through a hard time, we should be the first person they expect to show up. Hardships are opportunities for us to draw closer to the people we love, and when we understand how meaningful support is during tough times, showing up is easy.

- **Keep your promises:** When we say we're going to do something, we must follow through as often as possible. Actions speak louder than words when building trust. Even when we feel an impulse to avoid a commitment, we should keep our promises.

- **Consistently demonstrate integrity:** Sometimes doing the right thing isn't easy or comfortable. However, to build trust, it's essential to pride ourselves on consistently demonstrating integrity. This means being loyal and doing what's best for the relationship despite our own urges and desires.

- **Give your partner opportunities to show up for you:** Trust should always be mutual to benefit the relationship most. Rather than having a rigid, untrusting nature with our partners, we can loosen the reigns and let our partners show up for us how they intend to. Be open to unique expressions of care and support and accept these as positive signs of trustworthiness.

Trust is essential. However, we can build trust alongside our efforts to connect and cultivate closeness. It can also feel incredibly personal. To build trust in a way that aligns with your boundaries and beliefs, head to your Workbook and complete the exercise there. This will ensure that your efforts to build trust are not in vain, so you can move forward more authentically.

Solution 2: Non-sexual Intimacy

Intimacy is an essential part of a strong relationship. However, sex is only a small part of it. A powerful solution to cultivating closeness is focusing on non-sexual intimacy. This is the kind of intimacy that you may share with other relationships to produce deeper friendships or family bonds. However, in a romantic relationship, non-sexual intimacy can form a foundation where sexual intimacy can feel more fulfilling and meaningful.

To practice non-sexual intimacy, we can focus on:

- **Engaging with each of the 5 love languages. The 5 love languages** we discussed in the previous chapter are great ways to practice intimacy, regardless of our preferences. With thought and intention, we can use them to get closer to the people we love.

- **Staying present with others.** Our undivided attention can make any activity or conversation more intimate. We can stay present by grounding ourselves, managing our emotions, and constructively coping with avoidant impulses.

- **Offering emotional support.** Emotional support can deepen our connections dramatically in both good and bad times. For example, if a partner is starting a new project, we can show them emotional support by encouraging them, validating their aspirations, and asking to know more about their ideas. Or, if our partner is having a tough time, we can take time to listen to them, offer comfort, and validate their experience.

- **Initiating thoughtful conversations.** We don't have to be the best communicators to initiate meaningful conversations. A thoughtful conversation might include noticing how our partners get stressed every time they talk to a particular family member or bringing up our partner's new interests. Thoughtful conversations are about showing our partners that we notice intimate details about who they are and what impacts them.

- **Sharing our favorite things with others.** The things we like can reveal a lot about who we are. Sharing our favorite movies, interests, or hobbies can let others into our world, giving them the chance to feel closer to us. Allowing our partners to enjoy the things we enjoy is also a great way to feel accepted by them and squash the fear of rejection.

There are more ways to practice non-sexual intimacy, including many forms of non-sexual touch. Physical touch can be such a powerful solution to a lack of intimacy that we need to look at it separately.

Solution 3: Physical Touch

A gentle touch on the shoulder during a difficult conversation can mean the difference between division and connection. It can close the gap between two people, both physically and emotionally. Some forms of physical touch that encourage more intimacy in our relationships include:

- **Taking a loved one's hand.** Whether to initiate hand-holding or to comfort a crying friend, connecting hands is an incredibly intimate gesture that can communicate our care and connection instantly.

- **Leaning on each other.** There's something so subtly beautiful about resting a head on someone's shoulder. This form of physical touch can show someone that you trust them and feel safe enough to rest around them.

- **Putting an arm around someone.** Putting your arm around someone is a sweet way to feel more connected when spending time together. It can be most impactful when out in public and shows that you embrace the person even when others are around.

- **Cuddling.** Curling up on the couch after a long day is a great way to build emotional intimacy while enjoying the comfort of physical touch. Cuddling can vary in intensity depending on the nature of the relationship, making it a form of physical touch that can bring close friends, family, and romantic relationships a new level of closeness while enjoying movies or other cozy activities.

- **Sexual touch.** In a sexual relationship, we can exercise physical touch in new ways that may involve slowing down, becoming more present, and making an effort to connect emotionally rather than focusing only on physical connection. For example, including moments of eye contact, spending more time engaging in foreplay, or enjoying kissing and sexual touch that isn't a means to have sex.

If you feel uncomfortable with the idea of emotionally intimate physical touch or if another aspect of intimacy is triggering your avoidance, solution 4 comes in. As important as it is to learn what intimacy can include, it's equally as important to know how to execute it without allowing our avoidant impulses to stand in our way.

Solution 4: Peace Over Panic

As we discussed in Chapter 4, we may experience emotions and impulses that cause us to leave or avoid intimate situations. Avoidant attachment can make intimacy feel threatening and cause us to panic. This can look like any of the deactivating behaviors we discussed in Chapter 5. For this solution, we need to prioritize peace over panic so that our avoidant impulses and behaviors don't stop us from engaging intimately with others.

Chapters 4 and 5 are integral to quietening our avoidant impulses, but intimacy is a shared experience. The BEAR IT Technique is a powerful practice that we can use to capitalize on our panic. One of the most vulnerable and intimate things we can do is share our struggles with others. In the face of panic, we can open up to others and use our fear to cultivate closeness.

To prioritize peace over panic in a way that fully endorses intimacy, we can apply the BEAR IT Technique with an emphasis on letting others in. When we experience discomfort that pulls us out of the present, we can use this technique to ground us into intimacy. We can use it to make a gap in the fog that fear places around us so others can see through and show up for us. This is when a connection can extend beyond the surface level and become something beautiful.

Solution 5: Avoidant Self-Care

The fears and beliefs that keep us from intimately engaging with our partners often boil down to abandonment, rejection, or engulfment.[56] We may pride ourselves in independence and lean toward abandoning the relationship or rejecting closeness to cope with these fears. However, as people with avoidant attachments, it isn't fair to cope with these fears by completely denying our needs. Growing up avoidant leaves us with the need for more independence and alone time.

This doesn't have to be a bad thing.

Along this journey, as we push ourselves out of our comfort zones, we must account for these needs. Denying them completely is not healthy and may lead to a sense of burnout that causes our progress to backfire. That's why Solution 5 is avoidant self-care. Even though our needs may remove us from our relationships, there is a time and a place where that isn't such a bad thing.

Avoidant self-care may include:

- Taking structured alone time when needed, making sure to communicate this need clearly and preferably in advance.

- Allowing ourselves to take intimacy slowly, provided that our partner's understand our pacing and that we offer them enough reassurance of our care.

- Enjoying personal hobbies and interests while ensuring that our intentions are to regain energy and not escape our relationships.

- Allowing ourselves to say "no" when we're emotionally overwhelmed, while communicating our experience to our partners.

Becoming more comfortable in intimacy must be an empowering experience. For us to engage with others intimately, we need to approach it authentically. But we won't achieve that by disregarding our needs in favor of making others happy.

Healing avoidant attachment is not about learning to people please, but rather learning a healthy give-and-take between independence and connection. There is a term for this balance that we will discuss in Part 3, known as interdependence.

In secure relationships, autonomy is valuable. Both partners should strive for it together; it's not something that needs to be pursued alone. A healthy relationship will involve encouraging autonomy in others through support of personal interests and a true understanding and honoring of the other person's needs. These five solutions can help you cultivate the closeness needed to form such a deep understanding of one another.

CONCLUSION

Overcoming a fear of intimacy gradually warms our hearts as we allow others to step over our walls. Like a candle flame lighting another wick, intimacy is healing. With a willingness to be vulnerable, pushing beyond our fears can quickly shake avoidant attachment and encourage our relationships to grow and embrace longevity.

With the 5 Solutions in this chapter, we can practice intimacy in a way that is nourishing for ourselves and others. They encourage an approach to intimacy that is practical and include:

- Solution 1: Building trust with consistency and integrity.
- Solution 2: Prioritizing thoughtful non-sexual intimacy.
- Solution 3: Practicing emotionally intimate physical touch.
- Solution 4: Using the BEAR IT Technique to put peace over panic.
- Solution 5: Allowing ourselves the avoidant self-care necessary to feel empowered along this journey.

A fear of intimacy is the final layer of The Wall Of Detachment. Overcoming this fear and embracing intimacy in a way that feels good and sustainable for you is an extraordinary feat. It marks the crumbling of a wall that might have been up for years, keeping you alone, disconnected, and lonely.

I know how vulnerable it can feel to be standing without a wall up. I remember feeling exposed and at risk of hurt. But in this moment, I'll encourage you to forget about the hurt and think about the opportunity. Without your wall, you're open to the opportunity for deep, unbreakable love. You're open to friendship, connection, and a warm home among people who love you.

This milestone also marks the end of Part 2 and the beginning of a lot more. Having chipped away at The Wall Of Detachment, layer by layer, it's important that you learn to navigate life and relationships without all the protective mechanisms you had in place. In Part 3, we will explore ways to lay a new foundation for a lasting change in your attachment style. Turn the page now.

PART 3

A LASTING CHANGE

8

INDEPENDENCE AND INTERDEPENDENCE

Being Me While Being Together

"Two did not become one, but rather two came together–each one strong, healthy, and resilient, making the whole steadfast and true. They didn't lose themselves in each other, but found themselves in each other instead."

– Jennifer Lane

WHEN BOUNDARIES HOLD US BACK

Discomfort used to dictate where I placed my boundaries. I would exit relationships with more boundaries than I entered them with. The hurt and fear I experienced as a result of any conflict, even conflict that would be considered healthy, deepened my self-protective drive. Eventually, I was surrounded by a battlement of boundaries that I believed kept me safe.

Moving forward, new relationships became increasingly shallow, and I didn't completely understand why. Even my relationship with "the one that got away" wasn't as authentic as it felt. There was a reason I wasn't able to say yes to his proposal: I still had my wall up, and it had been up our entire relationship. In one way or another, I kept him at a distance, never allowing myself to fully commit to our love.

Boundaries were not a means to protect myself from mistreatment but rather from the risks of deep connection. I was too afraid of the pain that could come from loving someone wholeheartedly. I knew that the closer I drew to someone, the more painful it would be to lose them. And something in me believed I would lose them, no matter who they were or what I did.

I *had* to protect myself. And I thought rigid boundaries were the answer.

Before we continue, I want to clarify that boundaries are inherently a good thing. They are incredibly important in healthy relationships. In psychology, a boundary is a rule we set to demarcate where we end and another person begins. It is there to protect the integrity of a person in the pursuit of healthy, fulfilling relationships.[57]

However, not all boundaries are equal. When we set boundaries that restrict us from forming healthy connections, they are no longer good boundaries. When our boundaries serve to protect us in a way that hurts others, they can become unfair. Boundaries that are too rigid or limiting can even violate the boundaries and needs of others. They can hold us back in ways that sabotage good relationships by shutting others out.

Like an artery wall that keeps blood pumping to the heart, boundaries must be in favor of love. When they're too restricting, they cut off our life-giving supply. Good boundaries are stable enough to keep things flowing smoothly without causing unnecessary pain or distance. In avoidant attachment, our boundaries are generally too rigid, too many, or both. As we pull away and fight for our independence, we may adorn our Wall Of Detachment with a battlement of strong, rigid boundaries.

Independence And Interdependence

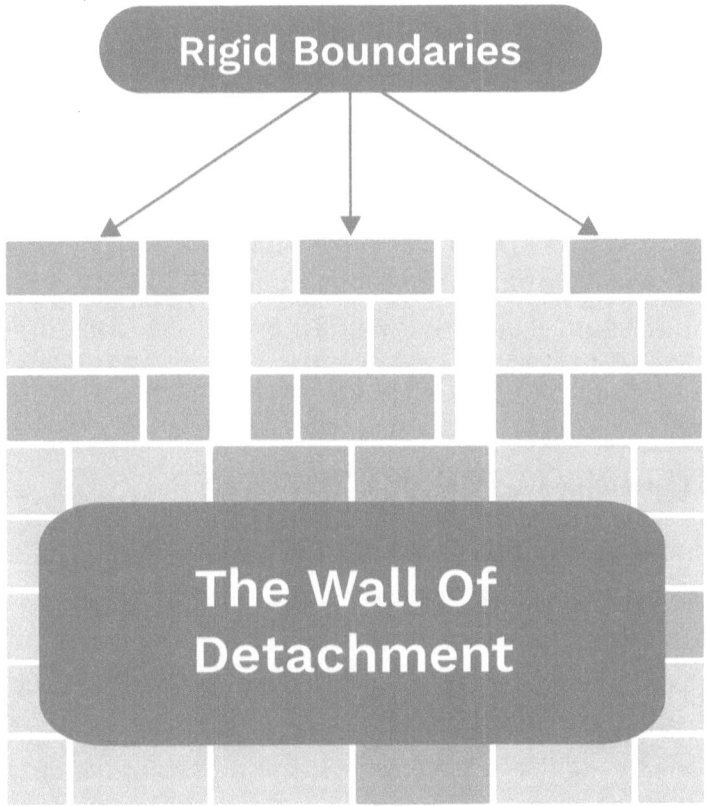

Rigid boundaries form a battelment that reinforces The Wall Of Detachment

Now that we are working to keep our personal Wall Of Detachment down, we need to address the battlement of boundaries we may have created around ourselves. As you can see in the diagram, a battlement is a segmented reinforcement built to protect a castle while allowing for defense. In avoidant attachment, the gaps allow us to fight for our independence while keeping others from reaching beyond our walls.

In this chapter, while I will encourage you to address your boundaries, I will not suggest that you break them down entirely. While I will help you embrace more secure connections, I will not suggest that you reject independence. Addressing our battlement of boundaries is not about allowing everyone in but rather about making sure there is enough space between our boundaries for others to love and connect with us. We will also discuss the importance of autonomy and how it can lead to secure connections when pursued productively.

MAINTAINING AUTONOMY TOGETHER

Independence is a healthy human need – when it's balanced. There's nothing wrong with wanting autonomy over your life and time alone. However, in avoidant attachment, we may lack the empathy necessary to fulfill our need for independence in a healthy and fair way. We may focus on what's best for us without truly considering the impact we have on those around us. This is where I'd like to propose a vital formula for the avoidant healing journey:

Autonomy + Empathy = Secure Connection

We can value autonomy without severing ties or damaging our relationships. We can even maintain autonomy in conjunction with our partner's autonomy. Autonomy is an essential need for everyone, regardless of whether or not we are in relationships. How we go about attaining it is what can set avoidant attachment apart from a secure attachment.

In avoidant attachment, we may fear that our partners become too dependent on us or that we may become too dependent on them. This fear is often what drives us to pursue independence with a sense of urgency. In this pursuit, we may forget to acknowledge our partner's experience as we suddenly pull back, exclude them from our plans, and comfortably remain behind our walls.

With each advancement toward connection that may threaten our complete independence, we may lay down another boundary. Unless we become aware of this pattern and find a way to embrace autonomy alongside our partners, our battlement of boundaries will leave little room for closeness and restrict our love gravely.

To maintain a sense of individuality while in a relationship, we must pursue something new. Instead of looking to build independence in our relationships, we can build interdependence. Interdependence is when two people in a relationship can rely on each other without negatively impacting their sense of self. An interdependent relationship will involve:[58]

- Healthy and fair boundaries that don't restrict our ability to love or accept love.

- Open, honest, and clear communication about needs, feelings, and the relationship.

- Taking responsibility for our behaviors and making a clear effort to remedy mistakes.

- Building a safe environment where both partners can be vulnerable and intimate.

- Enough room for both partners to maintain autonomy in their interests and goals.

- Two people with a willingness to depend on each other in appropriate ways without self-sacrificing or being overly demanding.

- Two people with a healthy self-esteem that doesn't fluctuate based on the state of the relationship.

In an interdependent relationship, we commit to mutually respect and appreciate each other's needs and boundaries. We actively build autonomy together. We will have a fair and balanced devotion to meeting our partner's needs while they show a fair and balanced devotion to meeting ours. To achieve an interdependent relationship while healing avoidant attachment, there are a few important steps we can take, including:

- Setting healthy boundaries without pushing people away.

- Communicating our needs and ensuring they are met.

- Exercising empathy in the way we manage relationships.

We will discuss the first two steps in this chapter which will cover the maintenance of autonomy in a secure connection. This will include thoughtful and practical ways to pursue interdependence. Then, in Chapters 9 and 10, we will explore empathy in its entirety including all the ways and places we can apply it.

As we continue, notice whether you feel any form of resistance to the idea of interdependence. If you do, I'd consider that completely normal. After spending a lifetime struggling with avoidant attachment, interdependence felt jarring to me. How you feel is valid, but don't let that stop you from giving these methods your all.

Set Healthy Boundaries Without Pushing People Away

Boundaries are an important part of an interdependent relationship because they will dictate how well we can pursue autonomy alongside our partners. Too many boundaries, or boundaries that are too rigid, won't leave enough room for our partners to weave their lives into ours. Our partners may look to us for connection at appropriate times like coming home from work, spending quality time together, or maintaining a household only for our battlement of boundaries to deflect their bids for connection.

Over time, boundaries that detract from healthy interdependence will create distance and disconnection in relationships. Our chronic pursuit of independence can earn us isolation and loneliness. To ensure our boundaries keep us comfortable in relationships while supporting interdependence, we can:

Balance Goals With Relationship Commitment

Our goals and aspirations are important aspects of our individuality. Many of our boundaries may involve protecting the time commitments associated with them. However, in avoidant attachment, we are likely to prioritize personal goals above our relationships in a way that creates feelings of neglect. Our rigid, goal-orientated boundaries may include:

- "Work comes first."
- "My relationships must not slow me down."

- "I'll never sacrifice my dreams for anyone."
- "I can't let emotions get in the way of progress."
- "I need to be alone to work towards my goals."

Time is a valuable resource in maintaining healthy relationships, which is why it's vital that we learn to balance time wisely and account for relationship commitments. We can gently shift our goal-related boundaries by:

- **Openly discussing our goals with our partners:** If they know what we're spending time on, they can support us and take our occasional distance less personally.

- **Getting involved with our partners' goals:** Asking about them, acknowledging them, and celebrating them can help our partners open up and feel supported.

- **Creating shared goals:** Shared goals combine our pursuit of goals and committed relationship time, creating ample bonding opportunities.

- **Setting aside time for goals and time for relationships:** Getting clear on how much time we spend working towards our goals and how much time we can commit to our relationships can help us avoid disappointment. However, we must communicate this arrangement with our partners to ensure that the time allocated for the relationship is adequate and fair.

Maintaining autonomy within a healthy relationship will require committing a fair portion of our time away from our personal goals and aspirations. However, with these tips in mind, we can find ways to connect with our partners while we pursue our goals. We can allow ourselves to slowly dissolve our rigid boundaries as we recognize that relationships can support our goals or at the very least, help us live more balanced lives.

Maintain Our Sense Of Individuality And Autonomy

As we mentioned earlier, in avoidant attachment, we may experience an urgency to maintain our sense of individuality and autonomy. This will often come in the form of a battlement of rigid boundaries that may include:

- "I won't share my feelings or personal details with anyone."
- "My personal time is non-negotiable. I need solitude."
- "I will always be completely independent."
- "My routine is going to stay the way it is."
- "I don't let my partner's needs disrupt my autonomy."
- "My beliefs are my beliefs, and no one can shake them."
- "This is who I am, and I will never change."

Many of us with avoidant attachment may believe that we will lose ourselves in relationships. However, to maintain our sense of identity and autonomy within a relationship, we can spend time getting clear on who we are through meditation and journaling. And it doesn't have to take long. Just 5 minutes of journaling daily can trigger new thoughts, give us insight into who we are, and help us feel more secure in relationships. The more we know ourselves, the less we can be influenced by others and the less we need to worry about feeling engulfed by the relationship.

A quick, daily meditation and/or journaling practice can add value to our much-needed alone time. Rather than using alone time to indulge in unhealthy distractions, we can recharge more productively. 5 minutes of meditation and/or journaling is enough to see a difference. It can include activities like:

- Answering 1 journal prompt. I've added a list of prompts you can try in your Workbook.

- Closing our eyes for 5 minutes while we take deep breaths and notice how we feel.

- Reflecting on journal entries from the past to gain a new perspective.

Meditation and journaling are powerful introspective practices to help us stay connected with ourselves regardless of the relationship we're in. Head to your Workbook now and try out a quick introspective exercise you can do daily to get to know yourself better and maintain a sense of identity.

Replace Restrictive Boundaries With Healthy Alternatives

With the previous two suggestions in mind, consider your current boundaries in relationships. Did you relate to any of the ones listed? Whether you did or not, there's an exercise in your Workbook that will help you identify which of your boundaries may be holding you back or hurting your relationships. Once you've identified at least 3 rigid boundaries, return here, and let's replace them together. Complete the Workbook exercise alongside these steps:

- **Step 1: Identify a rigid boundary.** We must take note of boundaries that restrict our relationships from healthy growth or those that were created to protect us from avoidant fears. For example, "This is who I am and I will never change." If you haven't already, use the prompts in your Workbook to help you with this step.

- **Step 2: Recognize the need behind the boundary.** For example, the boundary "This is who I am and I will never change" may mask a need for validation or independence because we may fear that we are being molded or asked to be someone we don't identify with. Ask yourself, what is this boundary trying to protect me from?

- **Step 3: Choose a new boundary.** The new boundary should fulfill the need without holding us back or hurting others. For example, we can change "This is who I am, and I will never change." to "My partners must respect me for who I am, even when I grow and change."

Boundaries are not meant to be soft or weak. They're there to protect us from being taken advantage of or mistreated. They're also there to help us assert ourselves and be treated the way we deserve. As you replace restrictive boundaries, don't shy away from boundaries that will help get your needs met. What's important is that they're strong enough to maintain your integrity without encouraging disconnection.

Communicate Your Needs And Boundaries To Ensure They Get Met

Building an interdependent relationship is not something that generally happens without some effort. Healthy relationships still require us to be clear about our needs to ensure they get met. We must determine what our needs are and who is responsible for meeting those needs. Humans are not built for complete independence. We thrive on connection, community, and helping each other.[59] Personal relationships are no different.

For people to thrive, we need each other. The sooner we accept that, the easier it becomes to accept help. We also don't need to fear engulfment when there is an equal exchange of energy. Interdependence allows us to help others while they help us, in a fair give-and-take.

Of course, this doesn't mean there won't be times when one half does more than the other. The goal is not to work out a perfect 50:50 ratio of meeting each other's needs daily. The goal is to create a dynamic where the give and take is balanced over time. This will require trust, understanding, and clear communication. But first, it requires clarity.

Clarifying Your Needs And Boundaries

You've clarified your boundaries in the previous exercise. Now let's uncover your needs in much the same way. Knowing our needs and boundaries will allow us to be very clear with our partners about what we need in a relationship so that our relationships can become safe and fulfilling. To clarify your needs, head to your Workbook one more time and answer at least 3 of these prompts with "I need, etc.":

- When I feel like withdrawing from a romantic relationship, what do I need to feel more secure?

- When I hesitate to express my ideas, thoughts, or feelings, what do I need that can help me feel more comfortable?

- When I feel overwhelmed by closeness or intimacy, what do I need to regain a sense of calm and continue the interaction?

- When I avoid conflict or difficult conversations, what do I need to help me feel safe enough to address the issue?

- When I feel under too much pressure in my relationships, what do I need to help release the pressure productively?

- When someone asks for more emotional vulnerability than I'm ready for, what do I need to help open up?

- In moments when I feel disconnected from my partner, what do I need to help me reconnect?

With clarity on at least 3 needs you have to feel fulfilled and understood in a relationship, the next step is to communicate these needs to your partner. This will include negotiating how to best meet the needs as a team and giving your partner the freedom to discuss their needs in return.

Communicating Needs And Boundaries

Remember, not all needs are ours to fulfill. Many needs will require healthy relationships, including needs like:

- "I need clarity about my partner's feelings.": Our partners will be responsible for communicating their feelings with us.

- "I need my privacy.": Our partners will be responsible for helping us fulfill this need by respecting our privacy.

- "I need reassurance that it's okay for me to take alone time.": Our partners must offer us this reassurance by understanding and respecting our need for alone time.

- "I need to feel supported in my personal goals.": Our partners will be responsible for listening to us and offering us the support we need.

- "I need trust in the relationship.": Our partners will need to help us build and maintain trust in the relationship by being honest and trustworthy.

For interdependence to form, we must have open communication in our relationships to discuss and negotiate needs. We can either initiate this conversation with our partners or be open to it if our partners initiate it first. The discussion should include:

- Asserting our needs to our partners.

- Discussing which needs we expect them to help us fulfill.

- Allowing our partners to negotiate with us based on their capacity to fulfill those needs.

- Allowing our partners to express their needs in return gives us the opportunity to listen and negotiate with them.

There is a reason this is a negotiation and not an instruction. We must be empathetic towards what our partners are willing and able to offer us. Although it may not be exactly what we or they want, negotiation can give life to understanding, tolerance, and acceptance. Even the most secure relationships are not perfect, and every relationship takes a willingness to communicate openly. We need to negotiate toward a more fulfilling relationship with both partners' ideals. To do this, we should abide by these communication tips and scripts:

- **Always use "I" statements to express our needs and boundaries.** For example, "I need total honesty, even when it's uncomfortable." This will ensure we don't accidentally trigger defensiveness in our partners as we take full responsibility for having the need.

- **Use open-ended questions and statements to discuss needs.** For example, "Your support after an argument would help me reconnect. How do you feel you could best support me without disregarding your experience?"

- **Negotiate needs with compassion and reassurance.** For example, if our partners feel upset by our need for alone time, we might say, "I understand how much my alone time may have hurt you in the past. Please know that it's only a need to recharge and not a personal need to be away from you. What would make meeting this need easier for you?"

- **Share our discomfort empathetically and negotiate solutions.** For example, if our partner's need is "I need more quality time," we might say, "I understand that more quality time is important to you. That need feels like a lot of pressure for me because it makes me think that I'll have to sacrifice other important time commitments. However, what if we started a new tradition where we have a date night every Friday?"

- **Listen actively.** We must ground ourselves and ensure we can listen without becoming reactive or distracted. When our partners share their solutions and requests, we must listen well to ensure our partners feel heard and understood.

Allow this conversation to be exhilarating as you intimately discuss meeting needs that may have gone unmet in the relationship. Unmet needs can cause conflict and distance between two otherwise compatible partners. This important discussion is a way to weave your and your partners relationship efforts together. This is the essence of interdependency.

It's not meant to be scary, it's meant to be exciting. Like a rollercoaster, there will be ups and downs, but as long as everyone is committed to staying put and enjoying the ride, the risks don't outweigh the joy of the journey.

CONCLUSION

Rigid boundaries are common in avoidant attachment and only serve to reinforce our Walls Of Detachment. We put them in place to help us maintain a sense of independence and autonomy in our relationships, but because they are so restrictive, they can suffocate a good connection. As we continue to keep our Walls Of Detachment down, we must make sure our battlement of boundaries isn't standing in our way of secure connection.

To build a secure connection, we need to focus our efforts on building interdependence rather than independence. This will allow us to fulfill our need for autonomy alongside our partners in a way that serves to connect us even at a distance. We can do this by:

- Setting healthy boundaries without pushing people away.
- Communicating our needs and ensuring they are met.
- Exercising empathy in the way we manage relationships.

In this chapter, we learned how to address rigid boundaries without sacrificing our independence entirely. We focused on the first aspect of the formula for secure connection: Autonomy. However, we didn't talk about empathy.

Even though the methods throughout this chapter exercised empathy and understanding, interdependent relationships are not perfect; they can still involve conflict, setbacks, and healing. Learning to navigate setbacks with grace and empathy will ensure that we continue healing in a way that nurtures secure attachment. Turn the page now and let's begin the final and arguably most challenging part of the avoidant journey: nurturing empathy, even in the face of setbacks.

SETBACKS AND HEALING

Old Habits Die Hard

"It is more rewarding to resolve a conflict than to dissolve a relationship."

– Josh McDowell

A STORY OF FAILURE: HOW I OVERCAME MY BIGGEST SETBACK EVER

Within seconds my husband became a shell of a man. We'd just received the news that his mother, who had been ill for some time, passed away in her sleep. Although he had been preparing for this day, they were close, and it tore him to pieces. I put my hand on his shoulder, and we cried. I had no idea it would soon tear our relationship apart.

In the weeks that followed, my husband had far less capacity. He would come home from work exhausted and struggle to keep up with our family routine. He would fall asleep in the living room most nights, and when we'd have our morning coffee together before waking the kids, he'd cry and talk through his grief. This was all understandable, and I felt we were handling the loss well. But one morning, as he sobbed and clutched onto my hand, I felt something disturbing.

Like a switch, I felt my empathy toward my partner disappear. The rawness of his pain and his constant need for support became a vortex, which I felt was sucking me into his misery. Although I had been feeling drained for some time, I didn't expect him to be his usual self. I had pulled all my strength to keep being as supportive as possible. But at that moment, I went cold.

After all my efforts to overcome avoidant attachment, it consumed me once again. But instead of fighting back, I rested comfortably behind my wall, abandoning my husband in his grief.

As the days went on, each layer of my Wall Of Detachment re-cemented itself. Physical intimacy had already dwindled, boring a hole in our relationship for emotional intimacy to slip away. Sleeping in soon replaced our morning window for vulnerable coffee talks. I started honoring my impulses to escape, withdraw, and isolate. I often felt irritated when I saw my husband looking sad or numb and struggled to find joy in our relationship. Then, as my wall solidified again, I started to believe that I could only find refuge from my stress alone.

My relationship with my husband was not built with this wall in place. It was built on openness, patience, understanding, and a willingness to sit in discomfort together. But in my avoidance, I left him alone in one of his darkest times. I'm still forgiving myself for it.

This is an important chapter along your healing journey. Because there will likely be times when the thoughts, emotions, impulses, and behaviors of avoidant attachment resurface. But what you must know is that this is not a failure. Our avoidant attachment is so deeply ingrained in how we are wired that intense stress can trigger it. However, without the awareness to recognize that we are slipping back into old patterns, we risk damaging our most precious relationships.

After this tremendous loss in our family, leaving my avoidance unchecked led to separation. My husband couldn't bear to live with someone so cold, heartless, and dismissive of his feelings. And I don't blame him. Caught up in my delusions, I agreed that he should leave. He moved into his own apartment, and we stayed civil. However, with him gone, there was no one to blame for my dissatisfied state. After a few months of letting my pride take precedence, I started to reflect.

Looking back on my life and the patterns of my past, I asked myself how I ended up alone again. It didn't take long before I realized what had happened. Thankfully, after learning and applying what I need to share with you in this chapter, my husband came back home. He managed to recover from my betrayal and abandonment and was willing to forgive me. It took time, but that was the least I could give him after what I'd done.

I am incredibly lucky to have a partner who is so understanding and forgiving. But when a relationship is fresh, or the hurt is too much, it's always possible to damage a relationship forever. And even when a relationship heals, we can't undo the hurt we caused. There will always be a scar. Prevention will always be better than cure.

This is why this chapter is very dear to me. I'm going to share the importance of awareness, including how to tell when our avoidant attachment is triggered so that we can take action before it's too late. I'll also share a setback recovery plan that we can apply in these times to help soothe our attachment wounds and move forward without damaging our relationships. Join me now as we focus on what it takes to move forward after breeches in trust, closeness, and healthy attachment.

SPOTTING THE SIGNS OF REEMERGING AVOIDANCE

In hindsight, there were warning signs. They could've been signs of other issues like chronic stress or depression, two things I have struggled with immensely in my life. However, when avoidance is in our wiring, stress and other normal life events can trigger avoidance. This is something we should expect and account for, even when we don't see or feel any drastic signs.

For example, feeling irritable with our partners may be a normal response to real stressors. However, when avoidance is our dominant attachment style, we need to be aware of how normal signs of stress can progress into harmful behavioral patterns.

It's important that we learn to spot any signs of reemerging avoidance, even when stress or other struggles can account for them. Some early warning signs of reemerging avoidance may include:

Mental And Emotional Signs

My sudden lack of empathy was not the first sign my avoidance was reemerging. There was a spectrum of mental and emotional signals indicating that I was running on empty. When I went cold, I now know that it was because I shut down. I'd already pushed myself too far, given too much, and done little to replenish my energy. Some of the signs I experienced, along with others that you may experience include:

- **Negative thoughts about our partners or the relationship:** This can start small and happen just after conflict, but left unacknowledged these thoughts may occur after minor inconveniences too. For example, we may start thinking thoughts like "They're so lazy!" when our partners forget to put their laundry away.

- **Harmful and unfair beliefs about our partners or the relationship:** Experiencing a lot of negative thoughts about our partners can slowly form negative and unfair beliefs about them. For example, if we often think critically about our partners' cleaning habits, we may start believing "My partner has no respect for our shared space."

- **Uncomfortable emotions triggered by our partners or the relationship:** With the previous two warning signs in place, we will likely experience uncomfortable emotions. For example, if we believe our partners "have no respect," then we might start to feel disgusted by them when they forget to pack their shoes neatly or resentful toward them because we perceive their mistakes as disrespect.

- **Increased insecurities about ourselves or the relationship:** We may experience insecurities in the relationship that make us question ourselves or the validity of the connection. For example, "This relationship is too good to be true", "I'm not cut out for relationships," or "What if my partner is planning to leave me?"

- **Emotional numbness during conflict or intimacy:** Emotional numbness during conflict or intimacy may be a sign that we are becoming overwhelmed by conflict or intimacy again, indicating a backslide into avoidant attachment. We may struggle to feel our emotions, understand our emotions, or express our emotions properly.

The mental and emotional symptoms we experience may be subtle, but our minds are powerful. Just as changing our thoughts is powerful enough to begin the healing process, leaving old negative thinking patterns untamed can lead to a total avoidant relapse where our Wall Of Detachment reemerges.

We must stay aware of our thoughts, beliefs, and emotions, even when we feel like we've grown so much. Life will continue to bring us new challenges that may cause old wounds and patterns to resurface. In your Workbook, there is an exercise where you can list your warning signs of reemerging avoidance, starting with your mental and emotional signs and continuing through to the next 2 types of signs.

Behavioral Signs

With thoughts and emotions often come impulses and behaviors. Even if we aren't aware of our thoughts or emotions, we can look back on our recent behavioral patterns as tangible evidence of our avoidance. Remember, alexithymia is a prevalent issue in avoidant attachment, where we may struggle to feel, understand, or express our emotions accurately. This is why a change in behavior may be the first obvious sign that avoidance is reemerging within us. As you read through these behavioral signs, continue adding to the list in your Workbook:

- **Resistance toward intimacy and closeness:** We may notice ourselves feeling more uncomfortable with basic physical or emotional intimacy, such as resistance toward hugs, kisses, or compliments. For example, upon reflection, I can recall feeling increasingly uncomfortable with kissing, only engaging in quick, closed-mouth kisses in the weeks before I suddenly went cold.

- **Holding back our thoughts in conflict:** If we notice ourselves holding thoughts back during conflict, it may be a sign that we are withdrawing rather than engaging. We may notice ourselves going quiet, suppressing our true feelings, or being selective with what we share in an attempt to keep the peace and avoid conflict.

- **Increased need for personal space:** When our avoidance is reemerging, we may experience an increased need for personal space. Remember, productive alone time is a form of self-care for avoidant attachment. In times of stress or anxiety, we will likely feel an impulse to be alone. While needing alone time is not a negative thing, an increased need for alone time is a warning sign we should not ignore along our healing journey.

- **Keeping conversations superficial:** Deep conversations about emotional needs, personal thoughts, or ambitions may become overwhelming. If we notice ourselves changing the subject in conversation to impersonal topics, like the weather or the news, we may be trying to divert the conversation away from us out of avoidance.

- **Masking our struggles or successes:** We may start to downplay our struggles or successes in conversation. For example, if someone asks us how we're doing, we may choose to tell a white lie to avoid attention or support. We may also choose to downplay our successes to avoid having to share more or gain attention.

- **Reverting to escapist coping mechanisms:** The way we cope is a powerful indicator of what's going on inside of us. When our avoidance is reemerging, we may start to favor escapist coping mechanisms like watching too much TV, drinking, or even overworking.

Reflecting on these behavioral warning signs, it's important to note that experiencing the impulse to engage in such behavior is enough of a warning sign. Even when we don't act on our avoidant impulses, we must acknowledge them and take action before impulses lead to deactivation.

Relationship Signs

A relationship is a constant give and take. If we upset the balance by exhibiting more avoidance, we will likely influence a change in our partners' behavior and the general relationship dynamic. Some relationship warning signs of reemerging avoidance may include:

- **Increased neediness and relationship anxiety in our partners:** Our partners will likely feel us pulling away. This may create a sense of relationship anxiety in them, increasing their neediness as our partners try and get their needs met.

- **Hearing our partners complain more than usual:** If we are withdrawing and spending more time alone, our partners may begin to feel abandoned and frustrated. Frustration and other difficult emotions can lead to more frequent complaints.

- **Noticing a lack of physical intimacy:** Our partners may not feel comfortable with physical intimacy when we've neglected our emotional connection through avoidant behaviors.

- **Receiving more check-ins from our partners:** Our partners may be the first to notice a shift in our behavior or demeanor. If we notice our partners initiating more check-ins like "Is everything okay?" or "Is something wrong?" we should pay attention.

- **Increased tension or conflict in the relationship:** Our delicate relationship dynamics can quickly shift in the face of stress, emotional disconnection, or distance. If our avoidance is reemerging, we will likely notice an increase in tension or conflict.

When we notice ourselves slipping back into old ways, with multiple warning signs going unaddressed, we should never ignore it. Even when it feels like "what's right", avoidant behavior is only going to lead to relationship destruction.

Looking back on my experience, I can now see how it was anything but sudden. I was exhausted. Inside I was emotionally withdrawn and irritable. Even though I was trying my best to show up for my partner, all I wanted was to get away. I needed alone time desperately, but I wasn't practicing the avoidant self-care that I used to. I ignored my own needs, overlooked many warning signs, and waited until it was too late. I waited until my relationship was hanging on by a hair before I realized what was going on.

It was only when I considered that my experience was related to avoidant attachment that I managed to turn things around. I had to backtrack fast or live in regret for the rest of my life. With the help of my therapist and a lot of accountability, I started my setback recovery plan and was lucky enough to save my relationship.

Things are bound to go wrong in life and in our relationships, but that doesn't mean we have to just turn our backs and let it be over.

With a setback recovery plan prepared, we can feel empowered to face challenges despite our reemerging avoidance. We can nip any old patterns in the bud and recenter ourselves on the path of connection. Let me share my setback recovery plan with you.

FOR WHEN THINGS GO WRONG: A PLAN FOR SETBACK RECOVERY

Once I'd realized that I'd single-handedly destroyed my marriage for no other reason than avoidant attachment, I was angry. I felt so angry at myself that I fell into a period of self-loathing. My kids watched me spiral down into anguish as I beat myself up for my mistake: pushing their father away in a time when loss should have brought us closer.

I entered a darkness that felt familiar. It was as if I'd been pulled back to the first time I'd heard about avoidant attachment. But this time, I hadn't just hurt myself and my partner, I'd hurt our kids as well. I felt powerless to do it once again. However, I had experience. Once I had the awareness that my avoidant attachment could return, and that it did, I went back to therapy. And this is what I learned:

Setbacks are inevitable.

However, setbacks are not failures, even though they may feel like it. How we respond is where we can hold ourselves accountable. Once I had been reminded of the tools I already had to overcome my avoidant thoughts, emotions, and behaviors, I started to recover. I slowly acknowledged what I'd been through and started implementing what I'd learned in a new way.

This is where I'll suggest that we put a setback recovery plan in place, to not only recover from reemerging avoidance but recognize it as early as possible. The more aware we are of our warning signs, and the better equipped we are to manage them, the less damage we will do.

At this point in the book, you already have the tools you need. What matters is how you continue to apply them. We must continue to heal and use what we've learned to stay secure in our relationships, no matter what triggers arise. Moving forward, this is the setback plan that I use and will suggest you implement too:

Step 1: Acknowledge The Warning Signs

If you're noticing tension in your relationship, or feel like something's shifting in you emotionally, the first step to setback recovery is acknowledging any warning signs. The sooner we can notice the warning signs of reemerging avoidant attachment, the sooner we can soothe them without damaging our relationships. Refer back to the list you made in your Workbook, and keep your warning signs in mind. Awareness is key here.

Step 2: Recognize The Trigger

Once we're aware that our avoidant tendencies are resurfacing, the next step is to recognize the trigger. Regardless of how subtle the warning sign is, something will always have caused it. Think back to Chapter 5 and the common triggers for avoidant impulses and behavior. These will also apply to setbacks in avoidant attachment.

What triggers our avoidance to reemerge will be highly subjective. What's important is that we are able to recognize what may have triggered our warning signs so we can address the issue appropriately. To do this, we can:

- Consider whether any recent or major changes occurred in our lives or in our partners' lives, such as the loss of a loved one, moving house, getting married, etc.

- Consider whether any long-term stressors have recently intensified. For example, if we have financial struggles, perhaps taking out a loan or paying off a car may trigger us.

- Consider past experiences where avoidant warning signs emerged and whether any recent events or circumstances may have reminded us of these experiences.

Sometimes, our triggers are subtle reminders of past traumatic events, or they may be obvious enough to recognize without much thought. Once you've acknowledged your warning signs, take time to reflect and recognize what may have triggered them.

Please note: If you are experiencing frequent, intense, or disturbing triggers related to past traumas and/or triggers accompanied by nightmares, long-lasting anxiety, and irritability, please consider seeking help from a mental health professional. These symptoms can be a sign of a number of anxiety, depression, or trauma-related disorders which can exacerbate attachment struggles and make healing more challenging.

Step 3: Meet The Need

We may not be able to change the circumstances that triggered our avoidant warning signs, but we can prevent our reemerging avoidance from damaging our relationships. How we manage setbacks matters. Even though we may have done a fair amount of rewiring to build resilience and gradually expose ourselves to discomfort, reemerging avoidance is a sign that we are dysregulated. We must care for ourselves accordingly in these times, in a way that is both self-compassionate and empathetic toward our partners.

Avoidant warning signs indicate unmet needs. Our attachment wounds may flare up and require soothing before we can continue functioning in a secure way. To meet our unmet needs, we must first identify them:

Mental And Emotional Needs:
- Emotional safety and trust
- Autonomy within the relationship
- Acceptance without pressure to change
- Reassurance and understanding
- Consistent and clear boundaries
- Predictability and control

Needs Underlying Impulses And Behaviors:
- Emotional validation

- Predictability and stability

- Clarity about expectations

- Alone time to regulate emotions

- Respected boundaries without guilt

Needs Underlying Relationship Tension:
- Interdependence

- Clear communication

- Non-intrusive support

- Emotional safety and trust

Once we understand the needs underlying our mental, emotional, behavioral, and relationship warning signs, we can work to meet these needs with compassion. We should refer back to the techniques and strategies throughout Part 2 to help meet these needs. However, we shouldn't try to meet them alone. Our partners have a key role to play in our continued healing.

Step 4: Involve Our Partners

To recover from setbacks effectively, we must let our partners in on what's happeneing. Helping them understand our change in behavior can give them a chance to support our recovery without taking our past mistakes personally. However, for our partners to support us, we must:

- **Communicate openly:** We can use "I" statements to share our experiences without causing misunderstandings. It's important that we are clear, straightforward, and open about the details. For example, "Lately, I've been feeling overwhelmed and feeling the urge to be alone. I'm sure it's because of the pressure I'm experiencing at work."

- **Apologize:** If we have already behaved in hurtful ways or said hurtful things, we must apologize to ensure that we begin healing the relationship. For example, "I'm so sorry for what I said yesterday. It wasn't fair or true. The truth is I'm overwhelmed and need to practice more self-care."

- **Accept help:** It's important to allow our partners to form part of our healing and recovery journey. Accepting help is a powerful opportunity to deepen our connection through vulnerability and intimacy.

When our partners are part of the process, we've already made major progress toward healing from a setback. Reemerging avoidant attachment aims toward disconnection, misunderstanding, and separation. Reconnecting with our partners in the middle of a setback is powerful. It will make moving forward more viable. In Chapter 10, we will explore more ways to involve our partners in our journey and in our lives.

Step 5: Move Forward

Finally, once we have addressed the setback alongside our partners, we can move forward. Don't let avoidance win. If given the space and time to do so, reemerging avoidance can envelop us. However, the sooner we move forward, the sooner we can repair any damage with a fresh track record. With the help of your partner, actively continue your healing journey by:

- Keeping your sights set on something positive in the relationship.

- Taking time to rest from triggering stressors as a team.

- Committing to regular quality time to support each other.

- Agreeing on set alone times that are fair and productive.

- Getting back on track with healing our Wall Of Detachment.

- Staying consistent to reestablish trust and connection.

Healing is going to include setbacks, regardless of how healthy our relationships are. Setbacks are normal, even in secure attachment. However, when our setbacks involve reemerging avoidance, we must act fast before irreversible damage is done. Because the nature of avoidance is to disconnect and detach, it's vital that we include our partners in this process. Letting them in on our experience can mean the difference between abandoning them in the dark or using the setback as an opportunity for relationship growth.

CONCLUSION

After building a healthy household alongside my husband, I thought my avoidance was cured. There were still things I'd do from time to time that were remnants of my old ways, but they were minor enough to brush aside. However, after the loss in our family, those minor remnants grew into all-consuming avoidance that sabotaged my marriage. I hurt the people I love most.

Avoidant attachment is something that can flare in times of stress. And it's something that can devastate good relationships if we're not aware of the warning signs. But with awareness and our setback recovery plan, we can save our relationships. We can find security again when we:

- Acknowledge the warning signs
- Recognize our triggers
- Meet the needs going unmet
- Involve our partners in our healing
- Keep moving forward

It was my greatest setback that led me to learn what I shared with you in this chapter. But it is also how I realized the importance of including our partners in our healing. I realized the power of teamwork. While we need to take responsibility for our own healing and do what it takes to overcome our fears, we don't have to do it alone. And we shouldn't.

As someone who grew up prioritizing independence, I did it because I felt like it was the most effective and practical way to be successful. But I was wrong. If you want to know why and how your partner may be your greatest asset in life, turn the page, and let's get very clear on one final component of overcoming avoidant attachment. Whether it's through friendship, family, or in the LearnWell Community, I can't stress the importance of support enough.

10

BEYOND MYSELF

Supporting Our Partners
And Loved Ones

"Coming together is a beginning. Keeping together is progress. Working together is success."

– Henry Ford

WHAT I WISH I'D SAID SOONER

To my love,

Even though I don't say it as often as I should, I love you, and you mean the world to me. I see everything you do for me, including the thoughtful gifts you leave in secret, the sweet notes you write on the kitchen whiteboard, and the looks of endearment you flash me during crowded family dinners.

I know I don't touch you enough, at least not in the way you wish would come naturally to me. I want you to feel loved. I'll try to be more open to the intricate intimacy of a growing relationship like ours. I'm trying, but this letter isn't about me. It's me acknowledging you. I'm saying I get it now: I'm not easy. I've pushed you away when you've needed me. I've left you on the sidelines of my life, never stopping to wonder how that might feel. And I've made you feel like a burden. Well, you're not. And I see that now.

I'm so incredibly sorry for any hurt that I've caused you. If you can find it in your heart to forgive me, I promise I will do better. With the insight I have now, I promise things will change. I'll be there for you when you need me and turn towards you in times of stress. We can be a team, like you always wanted.

I don't say these things in vain. My healing has brought me somewhere new. If I sincerely ask you to trust me this time, will you?

Yours truly

—

This is everything I wish I'd said sooner before my distance drove a hole in my partner's heart. If I'd said this while we were still together, maybe we would've had a chance. Maybe I wouldn't have torn our family apart. I spent years blaming him for leaving me. But in hindsight, I deserved it. Even though my actions were often driven by fear, I was selfish. My comfort was at his expense.

If I'd said this sooner, perhaps he would have afforded me the grace I so desperately needed. Although our relationship did heal, there will always be a scar. The wounds I inflicted will forever be a part of our story. That doesn't have to be a bad thing. Our story is one of redemption. But I'm still forgiving myself. However, despite the betrayal, pain, and healing, I learned the most valuable lesson I feel all avoidants must learn:

Connection is our greatest asset.

Whether we are currently in a relationship or not, the avoidantly attached person needs to understand the value of a healthy, secure relationship. Part of the avoidant struggle is believing relationships aren't worth the trouble. Even if we have never thought this thought, some part of us subconsciously avoids closeness out of fear or self-protection. We may feel that allowing a relationship to progress puts us at risk of burden, hurt, or dependency.

Although there is truth to these fears, I now understand that isn't the whole truth. We're only looking at one side of the equation. On the other side is love, joy, support, and more than enough to tip the scales and make the risk worth it.

If you're not already convinced that healing is worth a genuine try, let this chapter be your final compelling force. Let me show you exactly how and why connection is our greatest asset. Try the exercises throughout this chapter and experience the shift for yourself. I want you to experience the enlightening joy and ease teamwork introduces to your life. This may be the last chapter, but it's one of the most important. Give it all you've got.

THE VALUE OF TEAMWORK: HOW TO INCLUDE OUR PARTNERS IN OUR HEALING JOURNEY

By this point in the book, we've done a lot to demolish our Wall Of Detachment. We've worked on changing our mindset to allow for connection, building empathy, feeling our emotions, and regulating them before they spiral into deactivating behaviors. We've started facing our fears and engaging with more vulnerability.

Interdependence should now be our goal, and our plan to navigate setbacks successfully is in place. But what about our fundamental relationship tactic? What about our nature in relationships? Who are we healing for?

These questions are important. But as someone who lived for decades as an avoidantly attached person, let me give you my answer:

We strive for connection to fill a void within ourselves. Although we may want to be good partners, friends, and people, we ask ourselves, "What's in it for me?"

While this doesn't make us bad people, it does make us somewhat selfish. Selfishness is not always bad either because it can be resourceful. It can keep us protected, cared for, and in first place. But where does it leave others?

Being "me-orientated" helped me to stay in control and it helped me to get what I want. However, it's also why avoidance was able to submerge me again. I hadn't truly let it go. Fundamentally, I was still selfish. I was loving, supportive, and present in my relationship, but there were things I'd overlooked. My idea of teamwork was "Let's both support each other doing our own thing." when it should have been "Let's do the things that will support each other."

The problem with a selfish approach to healing and seeking security is that we may place the burden of sacrifice on others. If a decision is what's best for us and not for our relationship, who pays the price? Our partners will likely have to bend their lives and themselves around our decisions if they choose to keep the relationship going. And when love is involved, many people will gladly make sacrifices for the sake of their partners.

However, when only one person makes sacrifices, long-term relationship success is not on the cards. The relationship may have longevity, but longevity isn't the only measure of relationship success. Connection is another, if not the most important one. But connection only goes skin deep without teamwork.

Teamwork is a skill. It's something that both partners must agree on when deciding how to navigate the relationship best. It stems from recognizing that a relationship is more secure and impactful when two people become one entity.

Even though true teamwork does call for selflessness, it is proven to be the most effective route toward success.***[60] When two people are driven to do what's best for the relationship first, everyone wins. Everyone is protected, cared for, and in first place.

As we move through this chapter, I will encourage you to let your partner in. This chapter is intended for healing avoidant attachment with support. It's about teamwork and the many ways our partners can play a pivotal role in our journey.

Read through this chapter and show it to your partner. Tell them the things you wish you could say now. Don't wait until it's too late like I did. Even though I was able to save my marriage, there have been consequences. Healing such a major setback takes time. Again, prevention is better than cure. Let your partner be a part of your prevention plan.

How To Support An Avoidant Partner

Let's start on a powerful note. This section is here for our partners—the people who may be hurting and confused by our behavior. Read through it for validation, confirmation, and help to articulate the avoidant struggle. However, when you're ready, hand this information to your partner and humbly ask them to sit with it.

Avoidant Attachment In A Nutshell

In a nutshell, here are some points that someone in a relationship with an avoidantly attached person ought to know:

- **Avoidant attachment is in our wiring:** People with an avoidant attachment do not choose to be avoidant.

Attachment styles are generally formed in childhood and are based on the relationships we experienced and witnessed with close caregivers.

- **With support and genuine effort, we can heal:** As with any insecure attachment style, avoidant attachment can be improved with the right approach, consistency, and patience.

- **Avoidant attachment is not a lack of care:** People with an avoidant attachment pull back out of fear, overwhelm, or to protect their sense of identity, and not out of a lack of care.

- **Emotions and empathy may be a genuine struggle:** Our ability to feel, understand, and express emotions may be hindered. However, this doesn't mean we can't feel love or that we don't want to enjoy our relationships. We may just need more time to process our emotions fully and accurately.

- **Emotional overwhelm is a major trigger:** Intense emotions can overwhelm avoidant partners and lead to a shutdown response. This is often why we pull away, go quiet, or disengage during or after emotionally intense interactions.

- **Autonomy is not just a want, it's a need:** Independence is at the top of an avoidant's priority list. Whether formed in childhood or influenced later in life, an avoidant person learned that they must fend for themselves.

- **Needing space is not rejection:** When someone with an avoidant attachment style withdraws or takes space, it is generally a form of self-regulation and not rejection.

Tips For Supporting An Avoidant Partner

Although it may seem like an avoidantly attached person is independent, we still require emotional support from our partners. However, supporting us best may require a different approach. Here are some tips on how to support an avoidant partner:

- **Respect their need for space:** You can do this by holding back on text messages, constant check-ins, or physical contact when your partner is distant. Ask your partner what their boundaries are regarding space to gain clarity.

- **Focus on small, subtle gestures:** A little goes a long way when supporting an avoidant. Reach out in a way that involves zero pressure, expectations, or demands. For example, a simple message saying "I'm here when you're ready" may be enough.

- **Acknowledge their efforts:** Show appreciation for an avoidant's efforts to open up emotionally, no matter how small or subtle it is. It may be the encouragement they need to continue opening up.

- **Try not to force emotional openness:** Putting pressure on an avoidant person is the fastest way to overwhelm them. Understand that forcing vulnerability will likely only achieve the opposite results.

- **Don't take distance personally:** The way you respond to distance can mean the difference between helping your partner recover sooner or causing them to stay away longer. Try to understand that their distance is about self-regulation, not punishment.

- **Offer reassurance in simple, effective ways:** People with an avoidant attachment need reassurance to feel understood and relieved of pressure. For example, "It's okay, I understand that you need space.", "I respect your boundary about physical intimacy" or "I'd like to see you this weekend, but there's no pressure. Whenever you're ready."

- **Release any pressure for them to change quickly:** Growth takes time, regardless of our attachment styles. However, pressure may make an avoidantly attached person shut down or feel unable to continue their efforts. Be patient with them and celebrate their progress.

As someone in a relationship with an avoidantly attached person, you may have made a lot of effort to support your partner in the past. However, when effort is spent in the wrong places, it may go to waste. With a deeper understanding of your avoidant partner, you can adjust your approach to loving and caring for them. For example, giving an avoidant partner space *is* loving them. It's understanding their needs and supporting them the way they need to be supported.

This section has been about you, the partner of an avoidant, but the next section will require a team effort. So, let's continue together and dive into two very important aspects of a secure relationship: effective conflict resolution and fostering closeness as a team.

HOW TO ENGAGE, GET CLOSER, AND HEAL TOGETHER

I'm not going to continue putting words to the value of teamwork because I want you to *feel* it. Experience is the fastest way to gain expert knowledge. When we've lived something, it's easier to understand the nuances of the experience so that we can advocate for it ourselves. What I will offer you are easy, enjoyable exercises that you can try together.

Teamwork in a relationship is not just a mindset, it's a practical solution to navigating the relationship successfully, no matter how different the two partners are. Consider the exercises you learn next as habits that will lead the relationship into security. Whether you're experiencing conflict, finding ways to love each other better, or looking to refresh a distant spark, these exercises will help your relationship come alive.

Conflict Resolution As A Team

An effective conflict resolution strategy requires two people on the same page about managing conflict. While one person adjusting their approach can help tremendously, the best results are seen when both partners apply the same conflict resolution approach. To navigate conflict as a team and make it through with your connection intact, follow these steps:

Step 1: Shifting Into A Team Mindset

Both partners must adopt a team mindset. Effective conflict resolution starts with an "us vs. the problem" approach rather than a "me vs. you" approach.[61] When conflict arises, your aim should be to find a mutually beneficial solution. It is never about winning or being right.

Step 2: Give Each Other Grace

While working toward a solution, give each other grace. Grace is the missing link that can make open and honest communication feel more palatable and compassionate. Consider the communication techniques offered in Chapter 4, and add a little grace. It takes two people to engage in conflict, which makes both partners responsible for the situation.

There is value in acknowledging each other's mistakes, but don't linger on them for too long. As you talk things out with "I" statements, calm body language, and clarity, try the following to add a little grace:

- Assume your partner has good intentions.
- Take a deep breath before responding.
- Avoid personal attacks on each other's character.
- Stay focused on finding a solution together.
- Offer each other ample patience and understanding.
- Be quick to admit to mistakes and quick to offer forgiveness.
- Acknowledge each other's efforts to remedy things.

When we give each other grace during conflict we exit fight-or-flight mode. It allows us to move past hurt quicker and focus on repair. Remember that your partner is only human. They love you, and are acting on their self-protective instincts. Their intention is not to hurt you.

Step 3: Perfecting The Art Of Repair

Once each person has had their turn to express themselves and feel heard, let repair happen quickly. This means being ready and willing to apologize. However, just as we each have love languages, as discussed in Chapter 6, we have unique needs in conflict resolution. For example, some people feel that physical affection is the best remedy for conflict, while others may appreciate words of apology best.

To perfect the art of repair, become familiar with each other's repair needs. Reflect on the following conflict resolution strategies and discuss what you each appreciate most after conflict:

- **Words of apology:** Offering a sincere verbal apology, acknowledging the hurt, and showing understanding.

- **Physical affection:** Offering gentle, physical touch, hugs, or holding hands to show care and establish reconnection.

- **Quality time:** Spending quality time together after conflict, such as sitting down for lunch or enjoying an activity while tension eases.

- **Action:** This is the basis of *showing* someone we're sorry rather than saying so. It can include helping our partners with a task or remedying our mistakes with new actions.

- **Humor or lightheartedness:** Making a light-hearted joke or initiating a playful interaction after conflict to help break the tension quickly.

- **Space and time to process:** Offering each other space to process the conflict alone or in silence. Offering patience and respecting autonomy to process hurt alone is a valid form of repair.

Repair needs will include actions or phrases that feel soothing to your mind and body. If receiving a hug helps to reignite feelings of trust and comfort in you, it may be helpful to include hugs in your repair strategy. However, if you both have conflicting repair needs, try to agree on a combination of repair tactics that will ensure both partners feel equally soothed after conflict.

For example, if an avoidant partner needs words of apology and space to self-regulate after conflict, while their partner needs physical touch, as a team, this pair may decide to: Offer words of apology while holding hands followed by a hug and a set amount of time alone. What's important is that your repair strategy soothes both partners equally.

Coping with conflict securely and repairing in a way that is soothing to both partners is an essential habit for healthy relationship attachment. However, it is also the most challenging aspect of teamwork. But with that out of the way, the next exercises are all about fostering closeness and keeping your spark alive. You've done the hard work, now let's discuss joy.

The Power Of "We": Exercises To Foster Closeness

Relationships are our greatest asset because they can be our greatest source of support in hard times and our greatest source of joy. Like the old saying, "A problem shared is a problem halved, and joy shared is joy doubled," research shows a strong connection between healthy relationships and reduced stress levels.***[62]

To foster closeness and enjoy the countless benefits of a healthy partnership, we need to form habits that encourage teamwork and connection. These exercises are simple yet powerful enough to foster the kind of closeness needed for a secure connection.

The Check-In Ritual

Building and maintaining a strong connection involves consistent, quality interactions. In avoidant attachment, bite-sized vulnerability may be more sustainable and impactful. It may help avoidant partners stay close and connected without becoming overwhelmed. This is why spending daily quality time together may be more helpful than a weekly catch-up.

To effectively hold a deep understanding of our partners and their lives, choose a time each day to check in with each other. Turn it into a daily ritual of closeness where you both come together and share openly. To make the check-in ritual a habit that impacts your relationship, you can:

- Choose a time of day that is convenient for both partners.
- Take turns to openly share things that feel important, even the little things.

- Prioritize emotional regulation to create an emotionally safe space.

- Make room for any conflicts or challenges during this window.

- Try not to skip a day, even when nothing significant is going on in your lives.

- Allow for humor, fun, and a lot of grace. Focus on building authentic closeness that allows for personality and character to shine through.

- Add to the ritual in meaningful ways that draw both partners in. For example, have a coffee together, go for a walk, or talk during dinner.

A daily check-in doesn't have to be long. Even 10 minutes a day to check in and ask each other a few meaningful questions is enough to foster closeness. Some questions and prompts you might like to use during check-ins include:

- "How was your day? Did anything interesting happen?"

- "Name one positive thing I did today and one thing that I could work on."

- "If you could change one thing about today, what would it be?"

- "Is there anything on your mind you haven't shared yet?"

- "What was the highlight of your day?"

- "Are you looking forward to anything this week?"

After you've asked each other a few meaningful questions and been through your daily check-in, a nice way to end a session is with gratitude.

A Gratitude Circle

Starting a gratitude circle can be practiced as a stand-alone tradition or as a nice way to wrap up your daily check-in ritual. It's as simple as taking turns sharing 3 things each person is grateful for about the other. Although I'm suggesting this for couples, a gratitude circle can be practiced with the entire family.

A great place to practice a gratitude circle is around the dinner table, where the name gratitude circle originated. However, you can choose a place and time to practice that makes more sense for you and your family. For example, you may practice gratitude on car rides, at bedtime, or after conflict to help lighten the mood and nurture connection.

The Weekly Date Night Challenge

Secure relationships practice autonomy and interdependence. However, with busy schedules and life's ups and downs, it can be easy to neglect a good relationship. The weekly date night challenge is a fun habit that can not only forge closeness quickly but with longevity in mind. In all the seriousness and challenge of healing, there must be a balance. We must practice joy and allow it in our relationships freely. However, to do that may still take intention and effort.

To put the weekly date night challenge into practice:

- **Pick one day a week that suits both partners.** This day can change each week, with the agreement that there must be at least 1 night a week saved for one-on-one quality time.

- **Pick an activity that feels fun and exciting.** This is the perfect opportunity to try something new, like a new hobby, DIY project, or dinner recipe. Your workbook has a list of activities.

- **Limit distractions where possible.** Try to limit distractions like cell phones, TV, or other family members. For the best results, this time must be dedicated to the relationship.

The idea of the weekly date night challenge is to challenge each other by trying something new as a team each week. Do things that are fun, light-hearted, and a little out of your comfort zone.

This challenge is the perfect opportunity to build closeness. It promotes fun while creating a supportive space for handling setbacks and mistakes as a team. For example, when one of you spills the pasta sauce, you'll have to clean up and compromise together.

These exercises are excellent habits for secure, loving relationships. They can highlight the most advantageous aspects of connection. Partners working to overcome avoidant attachment must recognize the value of their relationship. They must genuinely believe that engaging in life as a team is beneficial. These healthy, teambuilding exercises can help reinforce this belief through positive relationship experiences and healthy challenges.

CONCLUSION

Teamwork will tie everything we've learned throughout this book together. Healing avoidant attachment is most successfully done alongside a partner who is supportive and understanding. We need a safe environment to make mistakes and practice healthier relationship habits. Positive experience is the most valuable way to learn that relationships are an asset worth working for.

Between letting our partners in on our healing journey, helping them understand how to best support us, and working with them to build closeness, we can move forward. We can continue to manage our Wall Of Detachment with a loving partner by our side.

Don't let positive, vulnerable experiences wait. Engage with your partner now, even if it scares you. Let them in on your journey with an open mind and make room for plenty of grace. We're all just learning along the way.

Now, before you close this book, turn the page for some final words of encouragement. Although this is the end of the final chapter, it's only the beginning of your journey.

IN 90 SECONDS YOU CAN MAKE A HUGE DIFFERENCE

If you feel we've deserved it, please take a moment to leave a review on Amazon.

Your feedback means the world to us. It helps us to improve and it means better learning experiences for all our readers.

We'd be so grateful to you for your review!

Thank you!
Thank you!
Thank you! ♥

CONCLUSION

Addressing avoidant attachment can be confronting and feel like a lot of work. It takes a tremendous amount of courage and care. That didn't stop you from reaching this point and learning what you've learned. I'm so grateful that you're here and incredibly proud of you.

I know how tough the challenge is and how much you have to fight for connection when avoidance is pulling you into isolation. But what I hope for most is that you see the value in it now.

After successfully working through all 3 Parts of this book, from understanding avoidant attachment, addressing each layer of The Wall Of Detachment, and learning how to make connections last, you are equipped to move forward with a sense of victory.

Your willingness to heal is clear.

I know the journey isn't easy, but connection is an asset you won't regret investing in. Now, all I ask is that you keep going! Don't let yourself slip back into old patterns like I did. Keep growing, healing, and striving for secure love. To encourage you further, here are some positive signs that you are making good progress:

- You've noticed a decrease in the amount and intensity of conflict.
- You no longer withdraw from conflict so quickly and are able to stay present.

- Your impulses no longer have the same hold over you and rarely manifest as behaviors.

- You find yourself sharing more in conversations and don't shy away from emotions.

- You notice and understand your emotions and can now express them more clearly.

- You feel more willing to accept support and no longer rely solely on yourself.

- Your boundaries are clearer and don't block opportunities for closeness.

- You've become far more empathetic and responsive to other's emotions.

- You're starting to feel increasingly comfortable with intimacy.

Any indication that your relationships or sense of fulfillment in relationships is improving is excellent progress. This is not a journey to be undertaken lightly. Consistency and small improvements matter most. Even if you hit setbacks, don't give up. Apply what you've learned and watch the water settle.

I am so grateful that you chose this book to help guide your healing. May my story be a testimony that it doesn't matter how badly you've messed up. If avoidant attachment is ruining an otherwise healthy relationship, we can and should do something about it. With this book on your shelf, there's nothing standing in your way.

We're not bad partners, and we do care. Let's prove it.

REFERENCES

1. Jeffry A. Simpson, W. Steven Rholes, 2017, Adult Attachment, Stress, and Romantic Relationships, Retrieved from: https://www.ncbi.nlm.nih.gov/pmc/articles/PMC4845754/
2. Cleveland Clinic, 2023, Attachment Styles, Retrieved from: https://my.clevelandclinic.org/health/articles/25170-attachment-styles
3. Kendra Cherry, MSEd and David Susman, PhD, 2023, 4 Types of Attachment Styles, Retrieved from: https://www.verywellmind.com/attachment-styles-2795344#
4. Katherine L. Fiori, Jessica Buthmann, and Christy A. Denckla, 2017, Crying and Attachment Style: The Role of Romantic Relationships, Retrieved from: https://scholarworks.waldenu.edu/cgi/viewcontent.cgi?article=1255&context=jsbhs
5. Katherine L. Fiori, Jessica Buthmann, and Christy A. Denckla, 2017, Crying and Attachment Style: The Role of Romantic Relationships, Retrieved from: https://scholarworks.waldenu.edu/cgi/viewcontent.cgi?article=1255&context=jsbhs
6. Elizabeth Hopper, 2017, Can You Cultivate a More Secure Attachment Style?, Retrieved from: https://greatergood.berkeley.edu/article/item/can_you_cultivate_a_more_secure_attachment_style
7. Zeynep Set, 2019, Potential Regulatory Elements Between Attachment Styles and Psychopathology: Rejection Sensitivity and Self-esteem, Retrieved from: https://www.ncbi.nlm.nih.gov/pmc/articles/PMC6732807/

8. Richard Schwartz and Jacqueline Olds, 2015, Rewarding ourselves with love, Retrieved from: https://hms.harvard.edu/news-events/publications-archive/brain/love-brain

9. Richard Schwartz and Jacqueline Olds, 2015, Rewarding ourselves with love, Retrieved from: https://hms.harvard.edu/news-events/publications-archive/brain/love-brain

10. Adam S. Smith, Manal Tabbaa, Kelly Lei, et al., 2015, Local oxytocin tempers anxiety by activating GABAA receptors in the hypothalamic paraventricular nucleus, Retrieved from: https://www.ncbi.nlm.nih.gov/pmc/articles/PMC4695278/#:~:text=Oxytocin%20(Oxt)%20treatment%20increased%20GABA,neuronal%20populations%20in%20the%20PVN.

11. Cleveland Clinic, 2015, Gamma-Aminobutyric Acid (GABA), Retrieved from: https://my.clevelandclinic.org/health/articles/22857-gamma-aminobutyric-acid-gaba

12. Erin Digitale, 2019, Making connections, Retrieved from: https://stanmed.stanford.edu/kids-autism-connect-hormone-treatment-vasopressin/

13. Stephanie Watson, 2023, Serotonin: The natural mood booster, Retrieved from: https://www.health.harvard.edu/mind-and-mood/serotonin-the-natural-mood-booster

14. Stephanie Watson, 2024, Dopamine: The pathway to pleasure, Retrieved from: https://www.health.harvard.edu/mind-and-mood/dopamine-the-pathway-to-pleasure

15. Atilgan Erozkan, 2016, The Link between Types of Attachment and Childhood Trauma, Retrieved from: https://files.eric.ed.gov/fulltext/EJ1099777.pdf

16. R. Chris Fraley, 2018, Adult Attachment Theory and Research, Retrieved from: https://labs.psychology.illinois.edu/~rcfraley/attachment.htm

References

17. Anna Drescher, Saul McLeod, PhD, and Julia Simkus, 2024, Avoidant Attachment Style: Causes, Signs, Triggers & How to Heal, Retrieved from: https://www.simplypsychology.org/avoidant-attachment-style.html

18. Hatice Deveci Şirin, 2017, The predictive power of adult attachment patterns on interpersonal cognitive distortions of University Students, Retrieved from: https://files.eric.ed.gov/fulltext/EJ1156267.pdf

19. Matt Puderbaugh and Prabhu D. Emmady, 2023, Neuroplasticity, Retrieved from: https://www.ncbi.nlm.nih.gov/books/NBK557811/

20. Daphne M. Davis, PhD, and Jeffrey A. Hayes, PhD, 2012, What are the benefits of mindfulness, Retrieved from: https://www.apa.org/monitor/2012/07-08/ce-corner

21. Anna Lardone, Marianna Liparoti, Pierpaolo Sorrentino, et al., 2018, Mindfulness Meditation Is Related to Long-Lasting Changes in Hippocampal Functional Topology during Resting State: A Magnetoencephalography Study, Retrieved from: https://www.ncbi.nlm.nih.gov/pmc/articles/PMC6312586/

22. Andrew E. Budson, MD, 2021, Can mindfulness change your brain?, Retrieved from: https://www.health.harvard.edu/blog/can-mindfulness-change-your-brain-202105132455

23. Hatice Deveci Şirin, 2017, The predictive power of adult attachment patterns on interpersonal cognitive distortions of University Students, Retrieved from: https://files.eric.ed.gov/fulltext/EJ1156267.pdf

24. Rebecca Joy Stanborough, MFA and Nicole Washington, DO, MPH, 2023, How to Change Negative Thinking with Cognitive Restructuring, Retrieved from: https://www.healthline.com/health/cognitive-restructuring#gathering-evidence

25. Rebecca Joy Stanborough, MFA and Nicole Washington, DO, MPH, 2023, How to Change Negative Thinking with Cognitive Restructuring, Retrieved from: https://www.healthline.com/health/cognitive-restructuring#gathering-evidence

26. Talk Plus, NIHCE, 2009, Cognitive Restructuring, Retrieved from: https://www.elft.nhs.uk/sites/default/files/2022-08/cognitive-restructuring.pdf

27. Bay Area CBT Center, 2014, 11 Interpersonal Schemas, Retrieved from: https://bayareacbtcenter.com/interpersonal-schemas/

28. IQWiG, 2022, In brief: Cognitive behavioral therapy (CBT), Retrieved from: https://www.ncbi.nlm.nih.gov/books/NBK279297/

29. IQWiG, 2022, In brief: Cognitive behavioral therapy (CBT), Retrieved from: https://www.ncbi.nlm.nih.gov/books/NBK279297/

30. Bay Area CBT Center, 2023, CBT Tips for Coping With Dismissive Avoidant Attachment, Retrieved from: https://bayareacbtcenter.com/evidence-based-cbt-tips-for-coping-with-dismissive-avoidant-attachment/

31. Darius Cikanavicius, 2020, Childhood Trauma and Your Inner Criticand What to Do, Retrieved from: https://psychcentral.com/blog/psychology-self/2020/01/trauma-inner-critic#1

32. Dan Brennan, MD, 2023, What Is Avoidant Attachment?, Retrieved from: https://www.webmd.com/parenting/what-is-avoidant-attachment

33. Hatice Deveci Şirin, 2017, The predictive power of adult attachment patterns on interpersonal cognitive distortions of University Students, Retrieved from: https://files.eric.ed.gov/fulltext/EJ1156267.pdf

34. Jayne Leonard, Timothy J. Legg, PhD, PsyD, 2023, What to know about alexithymia, Retrieved from: https://www.medicalnewstoday.com/articles/326451
35. Kelley Munger, PhD, LPC, NCC, ND, How Adult Attachment Styles Impact Stress Response, Retrieved from: http://fueledschools.org/blog/how-your-attachment-style-impacts-your-stress-response#:~:text=An%20avoidant%20attachment%20history%20might,calibrated%20toward%20high%2Denergy%20mobilization
36. Paula R. Pietromonaco and Sally I. Powers, 2015, Attachment and Health-Related Physiological Stress Processes, Retrieved from: https://www.ncbi.nlm.nih.gov/pmc/articles/PMC4341899/
37. Di Lorenzo Rosaria, Venturelli Giulia, Spiga Giulia, et al., 2019, Emotional intelligence, empathy and alexithymia: a cross-sectional survey on emotional competence in a group of nursing students, Retrieved from: https://www.ncbi.nlm.nih.gov/pmc/articles/PMC6625563/
38. Di Lorenzo Rosaria, Venturelli Giulia, Spiga Giulia, et al., 2019, Emotional intelligence, empathy and alexithymia: a cross-sectional survey on emotional competence in a group of nursing students, Retrieved from: https://www.ncbi.nlm.nih.gov/pmc/articles/PMC6625563/
39. Jessica Beer, Ph. D. and Alicia Nortje, Ph.D., 2023, What Is Nervous System Regulation & Why Is It Important?, Retrieved from: https://positivepsychology.com/nervous-system-regulation/#:~:text=In%20times%20of%20danger%20or,calmness%20(McEwen%2C%202007)
40. Jeremy Hogeveen and Jordan Grafman, 2021, Alexithymia, Retrieved from: https://www.ncbi.nlm.nih.gov/pmc/articles/PMC8456171/

41. Jeremy Hogeveen and Jordan Grafman, 2021, Alexithymia, Retrieved from: https://www.ncbi.nlm.nih.gov/pmc/articles/PMC8456171/

42. J. Alan Graham, Ph.D., 2023, Relationships: The Avoidant Style, Retrieved from: https://www.atlantacenterforcoupletherapy.com/relationships-the-avoidant-style

43. Sara Lindberg, M.Ed and Sabrina Romanoff, PsyD, 2024, What Is Emotional Numbness?, Retrieved from: https://www.verywellmind.com/emotional-numbing-symptoms-2797372#toc-treatment-for-emotional-numbness

44. Sara Lindberg, M.Ed and Sabrina Romanoff, PsyD, 2024, What Is Emotional Numbness?, Retrieved from: https://www.verywellmind.com/emotional-numbing-symptoms-2797372#toc-treatment-for-emotional-numbness

45. Lisa Tams, 2024, ABC's of changing your thoughts and feelings to change your behavior, Retrieved from: https://www.canr.msu.edu/news/abcs_of_changing_your_thoughts_and_feelings_in_order_to_change_your_behavio

46. Jonice Webb Ph.D., 2024, How to Become More Self-Aware and Why You Should, Retrieved from: https://www.psychologytoday.com/za/blog/childhood-emotional-neglect/202403/how-to-become-more-self-aware-and-why-you-should

47. Clara V. Murray, Juno Irma-Louise Jacobs, Adam J. Rock, et al., 2021, Attachment style, thought suppression, self-compassion and depression: Testing a serial mediation model, Retrieved from: https://www.ncbi.nlm.nih.gov/pmc/articles/PMC7808589/

48. Clara V. Murray, Juno Irma-Louise Jacobs, Adam J. Rock, et al., 2021, Attachment style, thought suppression, self-compassion and depression: Testing a serial mediation

References

model, Retrieved from: https://www.ncbi.nlm.nih.gov/pmc/articles/PMC7808589/

49. Cleveland Clinic, 2023, Deconstructing Stonewalling, Retrieved from: https://health.clevelandclinic.org/stonewalling-in-a-relationship

50. Paula Durlofsky, PhD, 2015, Signs of an Emotionally Abusive Relationship, Retrieved from: https://psychcentral.com/blog/signs-of-an-emotionally-abusive-relationship#1

51. Anna Drescher, Saul McLeod, PhD and Julia Simkus, 2024, Avoidant Attachment Style: Causes, Signs, Triggers & How to Heal, Retrieved from: https://www.simplypsychology.org/avoidant-attachment-style.html#Triggers-of-Avoidant-Attachment

52. DBT.tools and Marsha Linehan, 2024, Opposite Action Skill, Retrieved from: https://dbt.tools/emotional_regulation/opposite-action.php

53. Society of Clinical Psychology, 2017, What Is Exposure Therapy?, Retrieved from: https://www.apa.org/ptsd-guideline/patients-and-families/exposure-therapy

54. Society of Clinical Psychology, 2017, What Is Exposure Therapy?, Retrieved from: https://www.apa.org/ptsd-guideline/patients-and-families/exposure-therapy

55. Cara Gardenswartz Ph.D., 2024, Emotional Intimacy: The Key to a Resilient and Fulfilling Relationship, Retrieved from: https://www.psychologytoday.com/za/blog/the-discomfort-zone/202408/emotional-intimacy-the-key-to-a-resilient-and-fulfilling

56. Melissa Madeson, Ph.D. and Alicia Nortje, Ph.D., 2023, How to Overcome Fear of Abandonment: 6 Helpful Worksheets, Retrieved from: https://positivepsychology.com/fear-of-abandonment/

57. American Psychological Association, 2018, APA Dictionary of Psychology, Retrieved from: https://dictionary.apa.org/boundary

58. Jodi Clarke, MA, LPC/MHSP and Carly Snyder, MD, 2023, How to Build a Relationship Based on Interdependence, Retrieved from: https://www.verywellmind.com/how-to-build-a-relationship-based-on-interdependence-4161249#:~:text=Interdependence%20involves%20a%20balance%20of,in%20appropriate%20and%20meaningful%20ways

59. Bryan Parkhurst and Keith Tarvin, 2021, On Being Social Beings, Retrieved from: https://www.oberlin.edu/oberlin-center-convergence/oberlin-center-convergence/learning-communities/on-being-social-beings

60. Glenn Geher Ph.D., 2022, Love as Teamwork, Retrieved from: https://www.psychologytoday.com/intl/blog/darwins-subterranean-world/202211/love-teamwork

61. Himmelfarb Health Sciences Library, 2024, Team Dynamics: Handling Conflict, Retrieved from: https://guides.himmelfarb.gwu.edu/teamdynamics/handling-conflict

62. Megan R. Goldring, Federica Pinelli, and Niall Bolger, 2022, Shared Reality Can Reduce Stressor Reactivity, Retrieved from: https://www.ncbi.nlm.nih.gov/pmc/articles/PMC9093073/

www.ingramcontent.com/pod-product-compliance
Lightning Source LLC
Chambersburg PA
CBHW020413080526
44584CB00014B/1309